THE ART QUILT

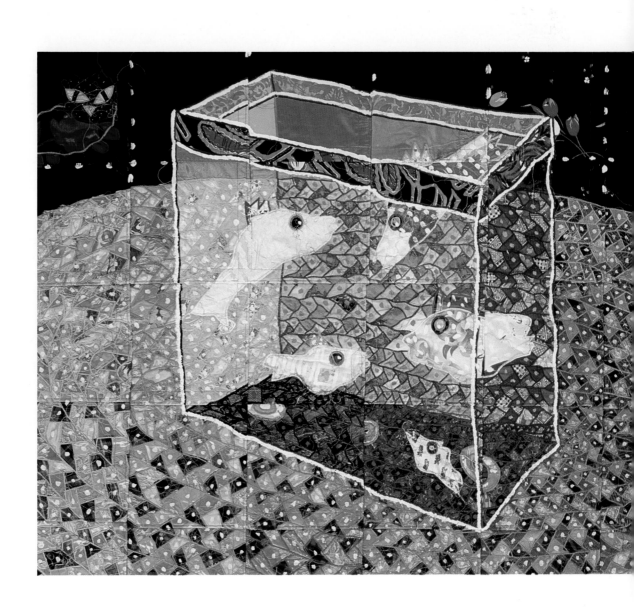

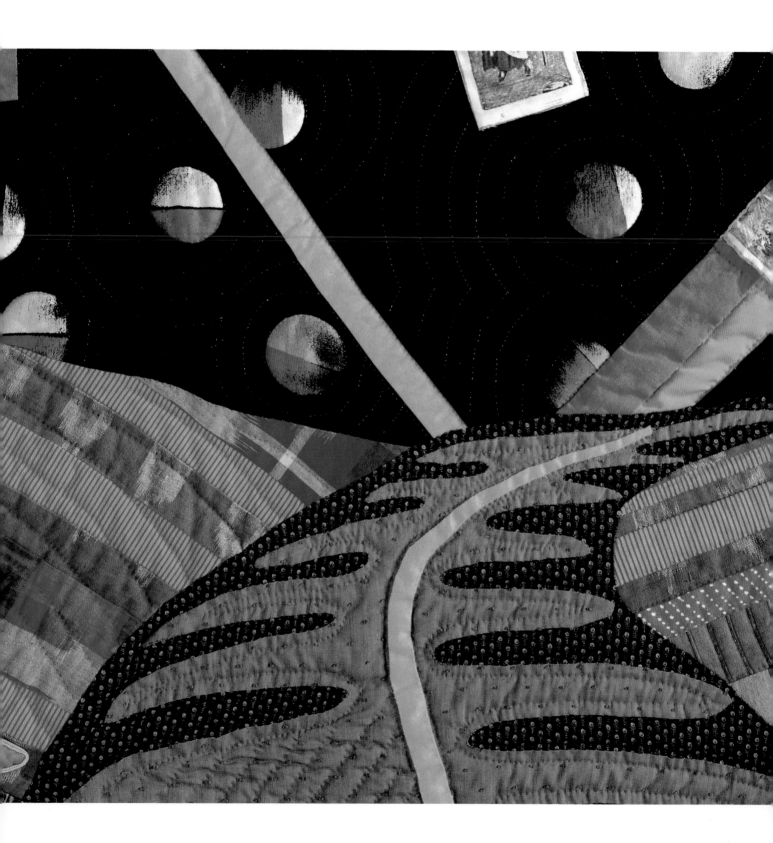

THE ART QUILT

PENNY McMORRIS
MICHAEL KILE

THE QUILT DIGEST PRESS
Simply the Best from NTC Publishing Group
Lincolnwood, Illinois U.S.A.

Editorial and production direction by Michael Kile.
Book Design by Kajun Graphics, San Francisco
Quilt photography by Sharon Risedorph unless otherwise credited.

Printed in Hong Kong

Preceding quilt details are from plates 24, 6, 19, 23, 20, and 24

Library of Congress Cataloging-in-Publication Data

McMorris, Penny
    The art quilt / Penny McMorris, Michael Kile
         p.   cm.
    Includes bibliographical references and index
    ISBN 0-8442-2649-1
    1. quilts–United States–History–20th century.
I. Kile, Michael, 1947-   II. Title
NK9112.M38 1996
746.46'0433'09048–dc20   95-51664
                                           CIP

1997 Printing

Published by The Quilt Digest Press,
a division of NTC Publishing Group,
4255 West Touhy Avenue,
Lincolnwood (Chicago), Illinois 60646-1975, U.S.A.

6 7 8 9 0 WKT 0 9 8 7 6 5 4 3

For Michael Kile

CONTENTS

Preface   13

Quilt Descriptions   16

The Art Quilt   21

The Quilts   71

Footnotes   126

Bibliography   129

Index   132

PREFACE

The *Art Quilt* was first published ten years ago to celebrate a new era in quilting. Writing a book on this emerging art form was the idea of my co-author, Michael Kile. Back in the early 1980s, Michael was an energetic young quilt dealer in partnership with Roderick Kiracofe in the San Francisco firm, Kiracofe and Kile. Since Michael loved both antique quilts and contemporary art, he was naturally fascinated by the bold new quilts he saw that broke away from quilting tradition. He and Rod featured some of these innovative quilts alongside antique quilts in a stylish new periodical they began publishing in 1983. It was called The Quilt Digest.

The idea for a full-length book on art quilts came to Michael that fall when the Director of the Los Angeles Municipal Art Gallery invited him to organize an exhibition of contemporary quilts. How he pulled that off I don't know. Undoubtedly his enthusiasm and his way with words got his foot into the right door at the right time. (I knew nothing about the planned show yet, for I didn't meet Michael until the following year.) The gallery's locale assured great media attention and a sophisticated, art-savvy audience. The space, built to showcase large-scale painting and sculpture, was perfect for monumental quilts. (If you've not visited the Los Angeles Municipal Gallery, visualize a space as open as an airplane hanger and you've got the picture.)

Michael wanted help in identifying quilt artists and in writing the manuscript for the book. He thought of me since he'd just seen my 1981 television series featuring interviews with contemporary quiltmakers. So, out of the blue, he called and invited me to help him. I jumped at the chance.

We set about listing possible quiltmakers, looking both for leading innovators and for emerging artists who seemed to have staying power. At the same time, I began my research for the book, hoping to set the new movement into the dual context of earlier quiltmaking and contemporary art.

In early 1984, Michael sent invitational letters to our wish list of quilt artists describing our goals for the show and book: "…There have been no exhibitions or books that have documented the role played by the 'trailblazers,' those quilt artists whose work challenges, demanding that those who view it look at quilts in new ways. Yes, these trailblazers have had their quilts included in many exhibitions, including all Quilt Nationals. But no curators or publishers have focused their undivided attentions upon this small group. That is, until now."

We invited the artists to create works especially for the show. Space being unlimited, we encouraged them to resist the temptation to make small, what I call "sofa-sized," quilts. "We would like for you to let your fantasies run wild," wrote Michael, whose fantasies knew no other way of running. "Create that quilt you have been dreaming about…we want large, looming works, as well as the more traditional pieces that hang flat against walls."

The opening was set for the evening of September 30, 1986. I still smile recalling Michael's delight in planning the opening reception, from the guest list (David Hockney was invited, but never showed), to the food (Martha Stewart could have taken lessons).

The opening was a resounding success, attended by thousands of invitees including 11 of the 16 artists in festive dress. Michael was splendid in a tux, while I wore, among other things, one of Michael's antique store finds: a black feather boa. The show packed in crowds throughout its run, breaking the gallery's attendance records and bringing in 1500 viewers on the last day alone.

Following the show, The Art Quilt traveled cross-country to seven other sites over the next three years. When the show finally closed, times had changed and the once firm boundaries between "art quilts" and "traditional quilts" had softened. Many more quilt artists were by then teaching classes and writing books that were reaching mainstream quiltmakers. And traditional quiltmakers were making increasingly innovative designs based on traditional themes.

Today, ten years after The Art Quilt was published and the show debuted, the quilting movement has matured and become a serious industry. There's even a great new quarterly, Art/Quilt Magazine, devoted entirely to these new quilts. Many of the artists featured in The Art Quilt have continued to lead the movement in serious ways. Yvonne Porcella, for example, recently founded a non-profit support organization called Studio Art Quilt Associates to foster professional growth and recognition for quilt artists. Nancy Crow, along with fellow quilt artist, Linda Fowler, holds an annual two-week Quilt Surface Design Symposium in Columbus, Ohio, every June, offering a wide range of advanced design classes. Nancy Crow and Ruth McDowell have both designed fabric lines and written books about their work. Michael James' work has merited both a traveling retrospective and a monograph.

If the museum world hasn't yet beaten a path to art quilters' doors, they've at least left their own doors open and are actively seeking gifts of quilts for their collections. And while serious private collectors are still a precious few, their patronage is making a real contribution and hopefully will continue and expand as others join the hunt, competing to collect the best art quilts.

I often wonder what my great friend Michael, who died in 1991, would write in this preface to his book's new edition. His memories would likely be sharper and wittier than mine. But I'm certain he'd want you to know that it all grew out of his great love for quilts, old and new, which is something I hope you'll feel as you turn the pages of The Art Quilt. From both of us — enjoy!

Penny McMorris

TERESE AGNEW, Milwaukee, Wisconsin.

Plate 26.

Proposed Deep Pit Mine Site, Lynne Township, Wisconsin, 80 × 73 inches. Terese is a sculptor whose quilts reflect her concern with three-dimensional space. She writes: "Many of my ideas come from daily walks…where the land is full of natural patterns. Recently, I have begun to include the context in which we see these places. Invariably, fields, gardens, and waterways are bounded by highways, parking lots, transmission towers, and air traffic. While the environment is widely discussed, I wonder how beauty can return to the discourse."

PAULINE BURBIDGE, Berwickshire, Scotland.

Plate 9.

Spirals I, 88 × 88 inches, completed in 1985, pieced and quilted by machine in cottons, some of which are hand-dyed. *Spirals I* and its companion quilt, *Spirals II,* based on spiral staircase images, compress a three-dimensional subject into a two-dimensional plane.

Plate 16.

Spirals II, 87½ × 84 inches, completed in 1985, pieced and quilted by machine in silks.

NANCY CROW, Baltimore, Ohio.

Plate 24.

Lady of Guadalupe, 81½ × 59 inches, completed in 1985, machine-pieced cottons and cotton blends. Hand-quilted by Sarah Hershberger, Holmesville, Ohio. While living in Mexico City as a student, Crow became familiar with this saint, and, in her words, "was fascinated by the idea of goodness radiating out from and around the form of Our Lady. In 1985, I felt a real need to produce quilts that reflected a sense of 'goodness.'"

DEBORAH J. FELIX, Atlantic Highlands, New Jersey.

Plate 22.

Discussing Plants for the Future, 69 × 90 inches, completed in 1985, hand-appliquéd and quilted by machine and hand in canvas and cotton blends, some painted and rubber-stamped by hand using textile paints. Signed in reverse appliqué. The title is a pun on discussing *plans* for the future.

VERONICA FITZGERALD, Oak Ridge, Tennessee.

Plate 23.

Untitled, 80 × 168½ inches, completed in 1985, pieced and appliquéd by machine in silks, cottons and rayons. Quilted by hand, partially by Mildred Quillen, Jacksboro, Tennessee.

GAYLE FRAAS AND DUNCAN SLADE, North Edgecomb, Maine.

Plate 4.

The Precipice, four panels, each 72 × 24 × 3 inches excluding projections, completed in 1986, each panel composed of an acrylic-painted plywood frame surrounding a cloth inset which is quilted by machine and hand in cotton, hand-painted with procion fiber-reactive dyes. Fraas and Slade live on the Maine coast and are, in their own words, "drawn to rocky shorelines at home and when we travel." *The Precipice* is at Point Sur on the California coast.

Plate 13.

Marsh Island, three panels, each measuring 78 × 48 × 3 inches excluding projections, with steps protruding 11¼ inches, and a 12 × 13½ inch urn atop the center panel, completed in 1986, each panel composed of an acrylic-painted plywood frame surrounding a cloth inset which is quilted by machine and hand in cotton, hand-painted with procion fiber-reactive dyes. Say the artists, "It seems we always seek out the nearest 'edge,' the ever-changing place in a landscape. Marsh Island, in Muscongus Bay off the Maine coast, has a small sandy beach with large rocks. As the tide recedes, fragments of pottery and dishes emerge from the sand."

JEAN HEWES, Fort Worth, Texas.

Plate 2.

Shooting Star, 87 × 121 inches, completed in 1985, pieced, appliquéd and quilted by machine in silks, wools, cotton batiks and cottons, some painted with dye. Signed and dated in machine embroidery.

Plate 8.

Angel, 87½ × 82 inches, completed in 1985, pieced, appliquéd and quilted by machine in silks, cotton batiks and cottons, some painted with dye. Embellished with sequins which are machine-strung but sewn by hand to the quilt. Signed and dated in machine embroidery.

Plate 12.

Dancers, 94 × 86 inches, made while living in Los Gatos, California in 1984, pieced, appliquéd and quilted by machine in silks, rayons, cotton batiks and cottons, some painted with dye. Indian and Afghan embroideries are employed. Signed and dated in machine embroidery.

MICHAEL JAMES, Somerset Village, Massachusetts.

Plate 1.

Rhythm/Color: Morris Men, 99½ × 99½ inches, completed and copyrighted in 1985, pieced and quilted by machine in cottons, cotton satins and silks. Signed and dated in embroidery. This quilt recalls the sudden, boisterous appearance of groups of colorfully costumed Morris dancers on village streets in England.

Plate 14.

Rhythm/Color: Improvisation, 99 × 99 inches, completed and copyrighted in 1985, pieced and quilted by machine in cottons, cotton satins and silks. Signed and dated in embroidery. This quilt is inspired by modern choreography.

M. JOAN LINTAULT, Carbondale, Illinois

Plate 27.

In the Grass, 91 × 98 inches. Joan Lintault is an internationally known fiber artist who teaches at Southern Illinois University in Carbondale. Her work is entirely hand dyed, printed, and painted. She writes: "In my work my objectives are to produce quilts that are inspired by nature. I choose flowers and insects because I want to bring perpetual summer indoors—the cool of the forest, the heat in the meadow, the whine of insects, and the sense of impending danger represented by the nasty things waiting in the grass."

RUTH B. McDOWELL, Winchester, Massachusetts.

Plate 10.

Waterlilies—Nymphaea odorata, 95 × 156 inches, completed and copyrighted in 1985, machine-pieced and hand-quilted cottons and cotton blends. Signed and dated in embroidery.

TERRIE HANCOCK MANGAT, Cincinnati, Ohio.

Plate 6.

Dashboard Saints: in memory of Saint Christopher (Who lost his magnetism…), 99 × 123 inches, completed in 1985, hand-appliquéd and machine-pieced cottons and cotton blends. Techniques include reverse appliqué, embroidery, beadwork and color photocopying. Embellished with a variety of ornaments. Hand-quilted by Sue Rule, Carlisle, Kentucky. Titled, signed and dated in embroidery. Mangat puts the viewer in the driver's seat, looking out into the road—and beyond—across a dashboard laden with plastic saint figurines. From the left, the figures are: St. Michael casting out the Devil, St. Francis of Assisi, Mary Magdalene, St. Theresa, St. Christopher, St. Valentine, the Virgin Mary and St. Peter. The saints are mourning the passing of two from their ranks who were de-sanctified by the Church: St. Christopher, seen here as a ghost, and St. Valentine, who has been cut up and floats into space. Says the artist, "I've often wondered what happened to the prayers offered to saints who were, the Church now tells us, never able to receive them."

Plate 15.

Mexican Graveyard, 106 × 86 inches, completed in 1985, hand-appliquéd and machine-pieced cottons, cotton blends, silks and linen canvas, with acrylic paint. Techniques include reverse appliqué, embroidery, beadwork and color photocopying. Embellished with various ornaments. Hand-quilted by Sue Rule, Carlisle, Kentucky. Signed and dated in embroidery.

Plate 25.

American Heritage Flea Market, 84½ × 70 inches, completed in 1986, hand appliquéd and pieced by hand and machine in cotton, cotton blends and silks, with acrylic paint. Techniques include reverse appliqué, embroidery, beadwork and color photocopying. Embellished with various ornaments. Hand-quilted by Sue Rule, Carlisle, Kentucky. Titled, signed and dated in embroidery.

THERESE MAY, San Jose, California.

Plate 3.

Thy Will Be Done, 88 × 91½ inches, completed in 1985, pieced and appliquéd by machine in cottons, velvets and taffetas, with acrylic paint. Tied by hand with yarn.

Plate 20.

For All the World to See, 85 × 89 inches, completed in 1984, pieced and appliquéd by machine in cottons, satins and velvets, with acrylic paint.

JAN MYERS-NEWBURY, Pittsburgh, Pennsylvania.

Plate 19.

Depth of Field III: Plane View, 84 × 131½ inches, completed in 1985, pieced and quilted by machine in cotton muslin which has been hand-dyed with procion fiber-reactive dyes. Made with the assistance of Joanne Olson, Richfield, Minnesota. Signed and dated in embroidery.

RISË NAGIN, Pittsburgh, Pennsylvania.

Plate 18.

On the Road with Marsden and Sonia, 75¼ × 97½ inches, completed in 1986, pieced, appliquéd and quilted by hand in silks, satins, cottons, polyesters and linen, with acrylic paint. This quilt reflects Nagin's admiration for artists Marsden Hartley and Sonia Delaunay.

YVONNE PORCELLA, Modesto, California.

Plate 7.

Snow on Mount Fuji, 132 × 86 × 14 inches, completed in 1985, machine-pieced and hand-quilted cottons, silks and metallic fabrics. Piecework can be seen on the inside of the foundation garment and on the outside of the decorative outer garment; close examination will reveal that the lining of the outer garment is hand-painted with textile paint.

JOAN SCHULZE, Sunnyvale, California.

Plate 11.

The Marriage: Woman/Man, 96 × 111 × 36 inches, *Woman* (96 × 81 inches) offset 30 inches to the right and 36 inches behind *Man* (96 × 80 inches), completed in 1985, hand-appliquéd and machine-pieced cottons, silks, nylons and mylar, some dyed or painted. Quilted by hand and machine. A portion of *Man* is dropped to reveal more of *Woman* because, says the artist, "A man eventually has to bend a bit if he has a strong wife."

Plate 17.

Self-Portrait, 92 × 73 inches, completed in 1985, machine-pieced and appliquéd and quilted by hand in cottons, silks and mylar, some dyed or painted. Techniques include cyanotyping and color photocopying. Signed and dated in embroidery. The box-like form on the quilt's front represents a chifforobe (a combined wardrobe and chest of drawers) the artist had as a child. The contents of the chifforobe, shown through its partially open door, represent that part of her inner life that she reveals to others.

PAMELA STUDSTILL, Pipe Creek, Texas.

Plate 5.

#49, 60½ × 84½ inches, completed in 1985, machine-pieced cottons, painted by hand. Hand-quilted by Bettie Studstill, Pipe Creek, Texas. Titled and signed in embroidery.

Plate 21.

#47, 60½ × 84½ inches, completed in 1985, machine-pieced cottons, painted by hand. Hand-quilted by Bettie Studstill, Pipe Creek, Texas. Titled and signed in embroidery.

THE ART QUILT

THE ART QUILT has emerged, and it heralds a dramatic and fundamental change in the history of quilts. Throughout the twentieth century, the quilts of our ancestors have enjoyed great popularity. They have been discovered, forgotten, then re-discovered by one excited generation after another. Most twentieth-century quiltmakers have demonstrated their affections for these antique quilts by sewing accurate renditions of them. But the art quilt is different from its predecessors: it is art for walls, not beds, created by artists abandoning media like painting, printmaking and ceramics to express themselves in original designs of cloth and thread. And while this new quilt owes its development to the current general enthusiasm for quilts, the original Arts and Crafts revival and the events which followed it contributed substantially to its emergence.

A typical late-Victorian interior, from a
Chicago home. Vintage photograph from The
Quilt Digest Press Collection.

S THE ARTS AND CRAFTS movement spread from
mid-nineteenth-century England to the United States,
it emphasized the use of natural, unadorned materials,
good workmanship and simple designs, gradually changing public taste. The decorative 1880's grew into the
tastefully simple 1900's. Women's magazines now recalled with dis-
taste the decorating styles of twenty years earlier. One columnist,
disdaining the 1880's, dubbed them the period "of gilded rolling-pins
and decorated snow shovels." Going on to describe a typical late-
Victorian room, she recalled, "Walls were covered with pictures.
Mantels and tables were hidden beneath 'drapes' and 'throws.' Rooms
were heavily curtained, and were made still darker by wall-papers of
dingy coloring. Picture frames were heavy with gold and plush. Bric-
à-brac was of the massive order."[1] One feverish home-decor re-
former went so far as to suggest that moral decay and divorce might
be caused by such decorative excess: "Who knows how much of
incompatibility of temper, sorrow, passionate discontent, mutual disgust, may not have grown out of these unhappy surroundings? Nay, . . .
divorce laws may be perhaps directly traced to some frightful in-
harmoniousness in wallpaper."[2] Another hinted that diseases lurked
amongst the knickknacks: "We have needless bric-a-brac, and the

24

dust and germs gather on objects which are supposed to be pretty when in fact they are most detestable."[3]

Young twentieth-century moderns rejected the ornate decorative taste of their parents. Instead, they followed William Morris's dictate to have nothing in the home that one did not know to be useful or believe to be beautiful. They decorated their homes comfortably but sparely. Bric-a-brac was banished. Whatnots? What for? Simplicity was the fashion. "We are weary of our burdens, our luxuries, our indulgences, and our amusements. All these superfluities are stale, and now we know better than ever, that the things which we once craved, are unprofitable. We are demanding something more rational.... The demand is for simplicity."[4] *Simplicity* meant straight-lined furniture, simple cotton curtains, handmade rugs on polished wood floors and, in the words of one early decorator, "plenty of optimism and white paint, comfortable chairs with lights beside them, open fires on the hearth and flowers wherever they 'belong', mirrors and sunshine in all rooms."[5] *House Beautiful* summed up the new simplicity, repeatedly endorsing the twin Arts and Crafts passwords—usefulness and beauty—that echo throughout the era: "The world has progressed since the early eighties, and in no field has the reformation been greater than in our homes.... We no longer fill our rooms with useless and unbeautiful things. We believe in a simpler, saner manner of living, and try to express it in our homes."[6]

As public taste moved away from the ornate toward the simple, people redecorated their homes, purchasing new items and re-discovering others which had been out of style during the late-Victorian era. Cotton quilts had been considered old-fashioned by the Victorians: while many women continued to make cotton patch-work, those who considered themselves up-to-date preferred their quilts to be as elaborate as their decor. Thus, quilts were dark, heavily embroidered, richly textured and patterned in intricate mosaic or *Crazy* designs. And the material these late-Victorian women selected for quilts, whether they lived in the city or on the farm, was the same material in which they chose to dress, if they could afford it: silk.[7]

As early as the 1880's, some commentators were anticipating the end of the silk *Crazy* fad and the revival of older quilt patterns. *Arthur's Home Magazine* noted, "Old patterns, and modifications of old ones, are continually coming to the front in silk quilts, so that when the crazy quilt has had its day there will be plenty of styles to supplant it."[8] Ten years later, *Ladies' Home Journal* announced that the cotton patchwork quilt was making a comeback: "The decree has gone forth that a revival of patchwork quilts is at hand, and dainty fingers whose owners have known only patches and patchwork from family description are busy placing the blocks together in new and artistic patterns, as well as in the real old-time order."[9] It was not long until the rankings of cotton quilts and silk quilts were completely reversed in the hierarchy of fashion. Silk quilts were viewed as fussy and overdone; pre-1870 cotton quilts were seen as precursors of Arts and Crafts simplicity. One needlework writer reflected the majority opinion of the period when she complained that quilting had "sunk to a very low level, from an artistic standpoint" during the late-Victorian era. The reason for this lack of artistry was, she said, the *Crazy* fad. She described the *Crazy* somewhat sourly as "the conglomerate collection of odd pieces of every color and quality, put together in what was well named 'crazy' manner."[10] Another writer, in a quilting brochure, reported a rumor that the first *Crazy* was made in an almshouse in Tewksbury, Massachusetts, by a "de-mented but gentle inmate, who delighted to sew together, in hap-hazard fashion, all the odd pieces given her."[11]

The Arts and Crafts movement did not intentionally set out to revive quilting, as it had embroidery,[12] but such a revival was, nevertheless, understandable as handmade crafts, the use of natural, unadorned materials and simple, straightforward designs were championed. "The arts-and-crafts movement has given dignity to even the humbler handicrafts," a *House Beautiful* writer condescended in 1904, but admitted, "the old quilts which are reappearing under such interesting circumstances are, many of them, quite worthy of their recall to consequence."[13] In fact, as the American Arts and Crafts movement enjoyed popularity, patchwork quilts were, for the first time, defined as art objects. The traditional boundary between the fine arts (like painting, drawing and sculpture) and the applied arts, or crafts (such as furniture making, needlework, pottery and weaving), was challenged. Fine artists began working in the crafts, making or designing useful objects because they found machine-produced goods ugly and poorly made. This involvement of the fine artist in the applied arts raised the status of all the crafts, quilts among them, in the eyes of impressionable critics and collectors. Now, the purpose of the finished object made less difference—whether it was to be hung on the wall and looked at, placed on the table and eaten off, or put on a bed and slept under. As long as an object was made with artistic intent, original ideas, good materials and techniques, it could be art. It was during this period that the first quilt collections were started, an important change in status for quilts, which had, until now, been looked upon by art and antique collectors as objects unworthy of display and safekeeping. Early quiltmakers were now written about as folk artists. One writer described them as "primitive people" who worked by "cutting from their scraps crude, but interesting, symbols which they sewed or appliquéd on to plain groundwork and quilted into useful and often beautiful quilts."[14] Not only were quilts collected during this period, but they were also written about as artistic objects. "When Patchwork Becomes an Art" was the title of a 1908 *Ladies' Home Journal* article describing five old quilts. Another article described a quilt as being "as exquisite and artistic as any embroidery," comparing quilts to a medium which had widely been acknowledged as an art form by the 1880's.[15] Marie Webster, whose book *Quilts: Their Story and How to Make Them* (1915) was the first full-length work devoted to quilts, wrote that "the work of the old-time quilters possesses artistic merit to a very high degree."[16] Webster, herself a very fine quiltmaker, produced some of the few quilts that could loosely be labeled as Arts and Crafts designs.

Left: "A Circus Bedquilt" by Maxfield Parrish, an illustration in the March 1905 issue of Ladies' Home Journal. A short text by the artist, containing recommendations to any quiltmaker considering his design, accompanied this illustration. Collection of Joyce Gross.

Right: A copy of "A Circus Bedquilt," made by Belle Gary, Gates Mills, Ohio, 1931, appliquéd cottons, without the aid of a pattern (no pattern was offered by the magazine). This quilt, made for a grandson, is similar to one made for a daughter in 1907, soon after the Parrish drawing was published. Collection of Dorothy G. Young, a daughter of the quiltmaker.

In 1905, *Ladies' Home Journal,* always an innovative proponent of Arts and Crafts taste, tried an interesting project for its readers. The magazine's editors adventurously commissioned five artists to develop original appliqué quilt designs, with hopes of reproducing the designs, in patterns, for their readers. Most of the designs were, however, far too complex for replication.[17] But, in the March 1905 issue, well-known artist Maxfield Parrish presented his usable drawings for "A Circus Bedquilt" (this page). Even *Needlecraft Magazine,* a monthly filled with how-to ideas, at times suggested quilting projects that required experimentation. In one issue, they suggested that their readers try stenciling original designs on their quilts. Into the 1920's, they would continue to emphasize a fresh approach to the medium: "The art of quilting…has become decidedly new again, since it is being applied in ways our foremothers never dreamed of.…We, of this modern generation, have greatly broadened its scope…; novel and delightful uses for it are continually being suggested."[18] This willingness to experiment was expounded by Arts and Crafts adherents who believed that new designs were just as valuable as old ones. "Design was once upon a time traditional; but the chain of tradition has snapped," wrote Arts and Crafts designer Lewis F. Day. Now, said Day, "one must study old work to see what has been done, and how it has been done, and then do one's own in one's own way."[19] What Day did not know was that the United States would soon enter another, totally different, period, following the Great War, in which a reverence for the past would predominate.

28

THE NEW ERA, known as the Colonial revival, fostered an interest in the arts, architecture and crafts of Colonial America. This interest (still with us today)[20] grew slowly from its beginnings at the Centennial Exposition held in Philadelphia in 1876, where American artifacts and antiques were displayed. Before the Colonial revival, popular styles of home decoration had borrowed designs eclectically from nearly every culture but our own. Up-to-date Victorian homes boasted a potpourri of such exotica as Chinese vases, Japanese screens and Turkish "cozy corners" which were furnished with low tables, imitation oil lamps, boldly patterned pillows and Oriental carpets. Victorian chair backs might have designs taken from French Gothic cathedral windows, and house designs could be borrowed from Greek temples, German castles or English inns. Knickknacks were collected—or copied—from everywhere. One from Egypt, via a Trenton, New Jersey, factory, was a two-foot-tall bust of Cleopatra, wearing a great deal of jewelry and not much else—a guaranteed conversation-starter in any Victorian parlor, to be sure.

Gradually, the idea spread that American art and antiques could be as valid a source of design inspiration as artifacts from other lands. People who were quick to recognize the artistry of Colonial antiques began scouring the countryside, buying superb examples for a few dollars.[21] By 1924, the Metropolitan Museum of Art in New York City had granted status to Colonial arts and crafts by devoting a new museum wing to displaying them. This certified that the Colonial revival was approved—and official. "It was a clarion call," recalls one writer on the appearance of Colonial arts in the Metropolitan. "Here were the art and handicrafts, the furniture and china and pewter and silver of our ancestors enshrined, catalogued, taken seriously, and displayed as treasure."[22] "Early American" became the unofficial national style, and even the A&P underwent a Colonial face lift. Suddenly, a great Colonial collecting boom began. "Day by day," announced an ad in *Good Housekeeping,* "the magic and beauty of Colonial America is making its way into the modern house."[23] One contemporary recalled that "every old farmhouse and barn [turned] into a potential treasure trove....Wagon wheels became ceiling fixtures; cobblers' benches became coffee tables; black caldrons and kettles hung on irons in fireplaces; Early American hand-blocked wallpapers were copied for machine production and sold by the mile. There was a boom in hand-hooked rugs, and you

A cover of Needlecraft Magazine *from the 1930's, demonstrating the influence of the Colonial revival. Collection of Bonnie Cready.*

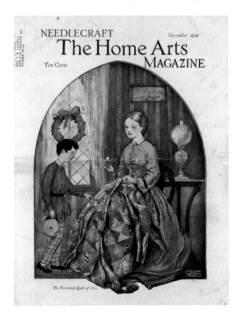

could buy them at New England filling stations when you paused for gas."[24]

Although interest in old quilts had been piqued by the Arts and Crafts movement, it was the Colonial revival that really put quilts back on the beds of mainstream America. Old quilts won release from their attic prisons. Women whose families had left them quilt-less were forced to either collect or make quilts in order to be in fashion. "The ambition of every possessor of a bedroom done in the popular Colonial manner is to own at least one piece of old-time calico patchwork for use as a counterpane," wrote Ruth Finley, whose classic 1929 book *Old Patchwork Quilts and the Women Who Made Them* was prompted by the renewed interest in quilts brought on by the Colonial revival. Finley admitted that the demand for patchwork was so great that "not only are modern quilts, designed after the old patterns, being made both by hand and machine, but yard goods... stamped or woven to represent pieced patchwork are procurable at most shops handling decorative materials."[25] By the 1930's, the amount of information available about quilts was catching up to the interest in them. While there were not yet the large quilt symposia with workshops and lectures, the national magazines devoted entirely to quilting or the hundreds of books that would be available half a century later, there was a large body of information for those women "eagerly searching for patterns typical of colonial days."[26] This literature undoubtedly kept women interested in quilting, just as it probably saved many quilts that formerly would have been "shoved off into the hired man's room or...used to blanket the horses."[27] The general public now knew more about quilts than ever before, and this increased knowledge fostered respect. "It was only a few years ago that the patchwork quilts made by our grandmothers were relegated to the attic, or given away, as being out of place in the modern bedroom," said the writer of a pamphlet on quiltmaking, "but now every woman who has one packed away is getting it out and displaying it as a treasured possession."[28]

While the Colonial revival can be credited with creating an enthusiasm for quilts, ensuring that many of them would be handed down to future generations, it also had a less desirable effect upon quilt-making. The Colonial revival moved quiltmaking away from original-ity and toward mere replication. Making a quilt became a matter of copying a printed pattern rather than thoughtfully adapting tradi-tional patterns or creating original designs. While experimentation in quiltmaking was encouraged, if in a limited way, during the Arts and Crafts era, mindless standardization became the norm during the Colonial revival. Without question, many inventive quilts were made during this period by women and men who abhorred the quilt-kit mindlessness that eventually dominated quiltmaking in the late 1930's, but these quilts are exceptions. For the most part, quilts were created according to directions handed down to quiltmakers by "experts." This rote copying violated the very spirit of the earlier Arts and Crafts movement—and of quiltmaking.

Commercial quilt patterns were not new when they gained in popularity in the 1920's and 1930's. The first quilt patterns appeared in the mid-nineteenth century, although commercial patterns for other types of needlework have existed since the 1520's.[29] These first quilt patterns were printed in farm newspapers and women's magazines such as *Godey's Lady's Book*. Later, during the 1880's, mail-order patterns were available from thread and fabric manufacturers. These firms found that women would pay money for thread and fabric scraps that normally would have been thrown away, using them to make crazy quilts and other fancywork. Eager to increase profits, the manufacturers advertised *Crazy* patterns in boldly printed ads, such as one that declared, "Ladies *Gone Crazy* over silk for patchwork."[30] Competition forced manufacturers to sweeten their offerings by adding full-size designs to trace and embroider and even pre-sewn *Crazy* blocks to decorate.

At the turn of the century, as the crazy quilt's popularity faded, manufacturers gradually began reviving old cotton patchwork patterns. The first known brochure of traditional pieced and appliquéd patterns appeared in 1898. It was published by Ladies Art Co., a St. Louis needlework supply firm. It featured 420 quilt patterns in a brochure entitled *Diagrams of Quilt Sofa and Pin Cushion Patterns* and promised the "prettiest, queerest, most grotesque, scarcest and original patterns."[31] Later, as the Colonial revival created an interest in traditional quilt patterns, dozens of brochures appeared. Most were printed between 1927 and 1939, at the height of this quilting revival. They were published by independent pattern publishers such as Home Art Studios, Colonial Pattern Co., McKim Studios and the before-mentioned Ladies Art Co., as well as quiltmaking supply firms. Certainly the fabric industry, which had watched helplessly as hemlines inched up and skirts slimmed down (a flapper's dress in 1928 needed only half the material used to make a 1918 dress),[32] saw

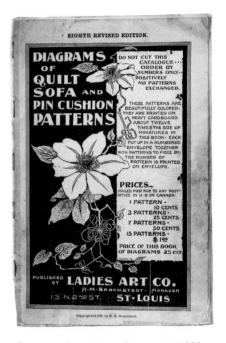

The cover of an edition of the original 1898 Ladies Art Co. brochure. Collection of George and Annette Amann.

a chance to increase sales by promoting patterns for quiltmaking. Competition among rival pattern manufacturers was fierce. "Avoid imitators" was a repeated warning in a Needlecraft Supply Co. brochure, *Patchwork Quilts: How to Make Them.* The introductory page boldly proclaimed, "We do not condemn honest competition—We welcome it." To those who read the smaller print following, they added, "But we despise cheap imitators who not only imitate our product but copy our ideas, our letters and our advertising...hoping to confuse the public."[33]

Newspapers and women's magazines also recognized the growing interest in quilts and began publishing quilt patterns regularly. At first, newspapers ran their own quiltmaking columns, but by the mid-thirties, as small newspapers fought to stay alive by running popular features, syndicated quilt-pattern columns appeared across the country.

In an attempt to attract quiltmakers, companies tried to make their patterns seem as appealing as possible. Since interest in Colonial patterns remained high, brochures and columns were written by fictional grandmas and aunts who assured readers that *their* patterns were authentically Colonial. Virginia Snow Studios boasted that their heirloom quilt blocks of "true Colonial character" had been gathered with the assistance of "Grandma Dexter."[34] (This busy senior citizen was also kept hard at work putting out Grandma Dexter's Quilting Twist thread, Grandma Dexter's Quilt Patches and crocheted bedspread patterns.) At W.L.M. Clark, Inc., later to become thread company Coats and Clark, "Grandmother Clark" was wracking her brain to remember all the patterns that "were the craze when I was a young girl, back in the Sixties."[35] The adjectives that run through these brochures and columns reinforce the romantic Colonial ideal: *old-timey, quaint, cozy, old-fashioned, homey.* No longer, it seems, did people think of quilts as *artistic.*

By the 1930's, old Colonial quilt patterns were still popular, but not exactly news. To keep the interest in quilts alive, professional pattern designers created new designs and re-named old patterns to follow current fads and fashions. The discovery in 1922 of King Tutankhamen's tomb, for example, set off an Egyptian craze. For years after, all of the decorative arts, quilts included, showed touches of Tut. New post offices, banks and movie palaces were graced with stone carvings in Egyptian motifs. Everyday items from earrings to cigarette cases sported scarabs and mummies. Grandmother Clark felt the call of the Nile and squared off the wings and body of a butterfly, making an *Egyptian Butterfly* pieced block in 1931.[36] There were also many quilt blocks reflecting the simultaneous interest in American Indian designs. As with the Egyptian motifs, the Indian themes possessed bold geometry that looked excitingly new and yet at the same time was old. The patterns—thunderbirds, zigzags and parallel bands of color, for example—resembled Art Deco motifs and seemed to many designers the perfect inspiration for quilt blocks. Indian-inspired quilt patterns appeared repeatedly throughout the 1930's in newspapers, magazines and quilting brochures.[37] And, as the public became increasingly familiar with Indian designs, seeing them in museum exhibitions, western movies and the press, an Indian look was fashioned by home decorators. Even the new Santa Fe *Super Chief* boasted a lounge car with Hopi motifs. Carrie Hall and Rose Kretsinger's still-popular 1935 book, *The Romance of the Patchwork Quilt,* suggested that anyone "charmed by a piece of Indian pottery or a blanket of Indian design" might like trying a pattern taken from an old Indian motif. The pattern suggested was *Swastika,* which World War II would soon erase from the contemporary quiltmaking vocabulary.

Left: Patterns available from Lockport Cotton Batting Company of Lockport, New York. In the lower left-hand corner is The Chief, *inspired by the interest in American Indian designs. Collection of Barbara Brackman.*

Right: A copy of The Chief, *maker unknown, c. 1945, found in Arizona, 95 × 78 inches, pieced cottons. Collection of Kay and Michael Magloff.*

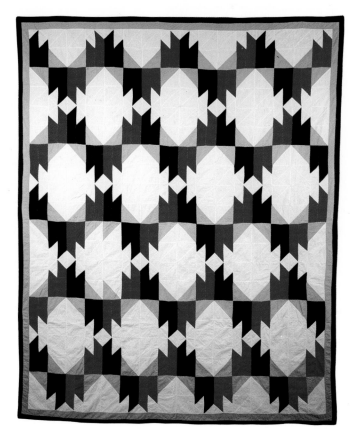

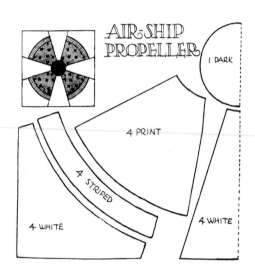

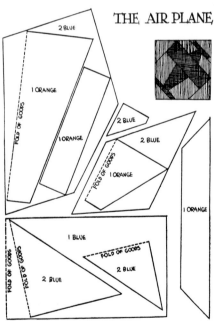

Top: Air-Ship Propeller, *a pattern published by* The Kansas City Star *in 1933. Collection of Barbara Brackman.*

Bottom: The Airplane, *a pattern published by* The Kansas City Star *in 1934. Collection of Barbara Brackman.*

New and re-named quilt blocks not only reflected an interest in the past but mirrored the interests of the day. This was a time that looked forward as intensely as it looked back, rewarding record-breaking speed, skill and endurance as exemplary of an exciting, prosperous future. Marathon dancing and flagpole sitting made headlines, and a full-speed-ahead spirit made "Faster, Faster!" a popular song of 1934. The adventurous exploits of Charles Lindbergh and Admiral Byrd made them heroes to a nation craving excitement. Byrd's dangerous Antarctic flight thrilled armchair adventurers and was commemorated by a *Byrd at the South Pole* block. And several quilt designers were inspired by Lindbergh's heroic 1927 solo crossing of the Atlantic.[38] One 1931 magazine even showed a snappy bathrobe designed from airplane quilt blocks.[39] The era's appetite for setting and breaking records sparked an informal competition among quiltmakers to see who could make the quilt containing the most pieces. One contender, who said she would rather quilt than eat, admitted that making her 21,840-piece quilt had proved a rather tedious chore. But she felt her efforts secured the record, making the experience worthwhile. As she told reporters, "I certainly pity the woman who beats that record, because I know how much work it takes." Records are, of course, made to be broken and it was not long before a nimble-needled gentleman named Albert Small equalled her 21,840 pieces and added another 100,000 before he was finished.[40]

Such popular thirties pastimes as playing games, doing puzzles and listening to the radio were celebrated in quilt designs. *The Kansas City Star* printed *The Four Winds*, named for the pieces in the popular game of mah jongg, and *Bridge Quilt* (facing page). The nation's addiction to crossword puzzles, which began in 1924 when the first book of the puzzles sold 750,000 copies, was reputed to have turned long ocean voyages into "protracted crossword orgies."[41] Hall and Kretsinger's book, in response, included a pattern of pieced squares titled, appropriately, *Crossword Puzzle.*[42] *The Kansas City Star* appealed to readers' interests with its *Ma Perkins Flower Garden*, a design named after the lead character in a popular radio serial.[43]

The poor state of the nation's economy during the Depression contributed to the popularity of quiltmaking. As late as 1937, President Roosevelt estimated that one-third of the nation still was "ill-fed, ill-housed, and ill-clad."[44] Without money for more expensive entertainments, many women turned to quiltmaking. Many of the quilt-block designs of this period can best be described as scrap-quilt designs, since they required many different small pieces of fabric. In keeping with the times, *The Kansas City Star* published *Economy* in 1933, *Depression* in 1937 and *Thrifty* and *The Thrifty Wife* in 1939, and a nationally syndicated quilt column (which bore the nom de plume "Nancy Cabot") printed two different patterns with the same grim title: *Hard Times Block*. Demonstrating the wide appeal of quilt-making during the Depression, twenty-five thousand quiltmakers entered a quilt contest sponsored by Sears, Roebuck at the 1933 Chicago World's Fair. Given the state of the economy, each entrant no doubt dreamed of winning the one-thousand-dollar first prize.

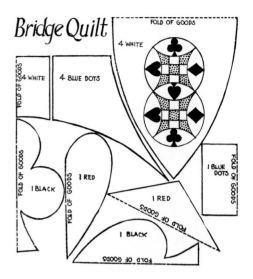

Bridge Quilt, *a pattern published by* The Kansas City Star *in 1933. Collection of Barbara Brackman.*

THE MODERN MOVEMENT in painting, graphic design, sculpture, architecture and industrial design during the 1920's and 1930's paid homage to the beauty of the machine. Paintings depicted skyscrapers and bridges; posters graphically celebrated the wonders of the past two decades: the radios and motion pictures, cars, planes and trains made by engineers—machine-age magicians harnessing the forces of nature to make life better than it had ever been before. One commentator wrote, "We fly faster, higher and farther than the birds. On steel rails we rush safely, behind giant horses of metal and fire. Ships large as palaces thrum across our seas. Our roads are alive with self-propelling conveyances so complex the most powerful prince could not have owned one a generation ago."[45] The creations of industrial designers—waffle irons, cash registers, alarm clocks and other appliances—were displayed on pedestals in art museums.[46]

By the late 1920's, the decorative arts emphasized a machine-like look that incorporated straight lines, hard edges and motifs of zigzags, rays of light and checkerboards. Art imitated machines rather than nature, in a style called Art Deco. Many quilt patterns of the period were given up-to-date names, but there was little in their designs to make them uniquely twentieth-century, linking them with the modern movements in art and design. There were examples of Art Deco influence, however. The purest of these were the stylized flower blocks of Ruby McKim that remain among the most innovative pieced patterns of all times. McKim was a needlework designer who had graduated from Parsons School of Design and become a syndicated columnist and the Art Needlework Editor for *Better*

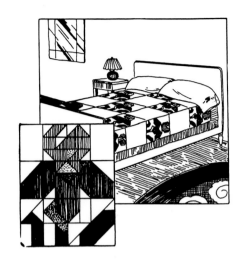

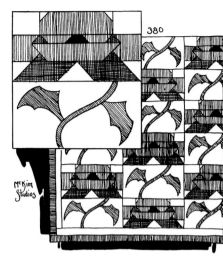

Three Ruby McKim patterns: Iris *(left),*
Poppy *(middle) and* Trumpet Vine *(right), as
illustrated in one of McKim Studios'* Designs
Worth Doing *catalogues. Collection of
Bonnie Cready.*

*A late-1930's advertisement displaying a
"streamlined" automobile. Collection of Marc
Neighbor.*

Homes and Gardens. She and her husband also operated their own
mail-order firm, McKim Studios, which published *One Hundred and
One Patchwork Patterns,* her 1931 compilation which was, and continues to be, widely distributed. They offered needlework kits and
designs through the mail in catalogues they called *Designs Worth
Doing.* Most of her catalogue items were rather standard fare—
embroidery designs of "cunning owls" and "jolly Russian dancers,"
frog-shaped doorstops and smart aprons in heart and flower shapes
("A woman must appear attractive while working to prepare the
food."[47]). But among the doorstops and embroidered pictures of
Mount Vernon was McKim's series of Art Deco–inspired flower patterns.[48] Her designs show one aspect of Art Deco design—a jazzy,
straight-lined, geometric look. But as the style developed, Art Deco
designs often exchanged their straight lines for flowing curves.

The impetus for curvilinear designs came from industry. Many
industrial designers tried to improve transportation during the Depression as a way of literally and symbolically getting the country
moving again. Their design experiments proved that cars, planes,
trains and boats with rounded edges could move faster than ones
with the old, squared-off, boxy shapes. This functional rounding,
which worked by reducing wind resistance, was called "streamlining."
By the early 1930's, streamlining was synonymous with progress.
Soon, as Russell Lynes observes, everything from toasters to refriger-
ators, from vacuum cleaners to orange-juice squeezers, became less
wind resistant.[49] Furniture was also gracefully streamlined, prompt-
ing one designer later in the decade to pun about rounding the
corner, referring to the post-Depression state of the economy as
well as to the corners of bureaus and tables. Fashion was also af-

36

fected. An ad in *Vogue's* April 1932 issue announced, "Spring styles say... 'CURVES!'"[50] The straight-lined, slim-hipped, flat-chested flappers of the twenties suddenly became what one magazine described as "Junoesque...with rounded naturally curved *derrières.*"[51] One social critic recalled that "one might almost have thought a new anatomical species had come into being."[52]

This change from the straight line to the curve is amply demonstrated in the quilts of the period. The best-loved pieced designs utilized curves: *Dresden Plate, Double Wedding Ring* and *Grandmother's Flower Garden.*[53] In appliqué quilts, even the normally straight quilt edge often curved into scallops, and the bodies of these quilts brimmed with rounded motifs. There were chubby sunbonnet girls and garlands of roses, overflowing cornucopias and lavish ribbon-tied bouquets, swags and sashes, serpentine vines heavy with grapes, and baskets spilling over with bluebells, sweet peas, poppies and irises, all inspected by butterflies and plump doves. Such luxuriant abundance, in fruit and flower colors of apricot, tangerine, peach, lemon, honeydew, violet, lilac, orchid and rose, must have seemed to its creators as just the right antidote for the Depression.

Iris, by Hannah Haynes Headlee, Topeka, Kansas, c. 1935–1940, 89 × 76 inches, appliquéd cottons, one of which is hand-dyed. An originally designed quilt exemplary of the finest work of its period. Collection of Sarah E. MacNeil. Courtesy of Marie Shirer.

IN DECEMBER 1941 the United States entered World War I By 1945, when the war ended, the country had been uprooted and the quilt revival was essentially at an end. The popularity that quiltmaking had enjoyed during the twenties and thirties had faded, a casualty, in part, of circumstances beyond its control. Although many women continued to make quilts during the late forties and the fifties, many more found they had neither the time nor need to quilt. More women than ever before had jobs outside the home, leaving them with less time to make quilts. The war had created new jobs and, at the same time, removed many men from the work force. Women stepped in to fill these job vacancies and many kept their new jobs after the war. There were twice as many women with government jobs in 1945, for example, as there had been in 1940. And many women who stayed at home had their hands full thanks to a predictable post-war baby boom. Besides, quilts were, for many, reminders of the Depression, a time when saving fabric scraps was often a necessity. One 1940's writer hinted at this when she wrote, "In this modern age of swift movement most of us do not take the time or have the patience to enter into the actual work of construction or quilting. We can easily purchase our machine made quilts in stores. For these reasons the art of quilting is dying."[54]

Quiltmaking was dying, however, for another reason. As previously noted, during the Depression the quilting industry had turned this innovative medium into a boring, mindless pastime. Professional designers made the creative decisions, leaving women with only the work of sewing the preordained quilts together. Companies printed patterns which determined size. Then, patterns were printed in color to, as "Grandma Dexter" put it, "assist the quilt maker in developing attractive color schemes."[55] It was not long before manufacturers were not only selecting designs and colors but cutting out the pieces and packaging the whole into kits they christened "ready-cut" quilts.[56] These labor-saving inventions, cousins to the new cake mixes and instant puddings, removed creativity from quiltmaking. With the introduction of these kits, quiltmaking became as far removed from art as are paint-by-number paintings.

Some contemporary writers questioned the effect that commercial quilt kits would have upon quiltmaking. Carrie Hall wrote, "In the

A pillow-top kit, complete with templates (foreground). Collection of Bonnie Cready.

ready-cut quilts offered for sale are seen the effects of this hurrying age in which we live."[57] But, at the same time, Hall herself suggested that quiltmakers turn their finished quilt tops over to experienced quilters for quilting, and called old quilts "an inspiration for imitation."[58] Now seeming more like a tedious task than a creative art, quiltmaking lost its audience after World War II.

Not much was written about quilts during the late 1940's and throughout the 1950's and early 1960's. While some original designs were made during this period, they were exceptions. Most quilts that were made followed traditional patterns or were made from kits. But women who wanted to express their creativity found no enjoyment in putting together the pieces cut for them from someone else's design. One woman recalled her experience with a quilt kit that she had purchased while recovering from an illness in 1956: "I bought one of those 'packaged quilts'—precut, prestamped, complete with threads, and the like. It seemed like a suitable occupation for a convalescent, needing no thought and only a witless putting in of stitches. . . . I soon quit the project in disgust, because it was so ugly and without taste." She declared that quilting was a lost art.[59]

The fifties were prosperous, optimistic times for most Americans. The country, recovering from a war, had no idea that it would soon be entering two others. Peacetime industry was booming and the days of scrimping were over. Products which promised to make our lives easier, our families happier and our faces prettier spilled out of tempting, colorful magazine ads like fruit from a cornucopia. It was an age of frills and luxury, when women could buy mink-handled beer-can openers from B. Altman's in New York City, shop with fourteen-carat-gold charge cards in California, buy whisky-flavored toothpaste and have their hair tinted in shades called Sparkling Sherry and Champagne Beige. Television antennas became the new status symbol, and the t.v. dinner was born. The fifties were a time of white bucks and coonskin caps, of "Purple People Eaters" and the mock-rodent trio "The Chipmunks." The fifties were, as the nostalgic television hit comedy recalling the period would later be called, *Happy Days*. But the fifties never prepared us for what was to come.

THE SIXTIES BEGAN with the highest hopes and aspirations. John F. Kennedy was elected President in 1960 and declared that an energetic new age had begun. The youthful new President demanded hard work and dedication, also promising an expedition to the moon in a race to beat the Russians. Martin Luther King, Jr. led blacks in a movement to earn long-promised, never-fulfilled freedoms. Most Americans, safe, prosperous but slightly discontented after the apathy of the fifties, were ready for a challenge. Not only was the political climate new in the early sixties, but so was everyday life for the average American. The fifties had ushered in an interest in "the younger generation." American culture, which had since the late nineteenth century centered much of its attention on children, began to cater obsequiously to the whims and desires of its younger set. America was obsessed with youth. The sock hops of the fifties were eclipsed by Chubby Checker and the twist. And when the Beatles arrived in New York City in February 1964, some Americans realized that life would never be quite the same.

The early sixties marked the emergence of California as the arbiter of popular American taste and from Berkeley came the free speech and attendant hippie movements. By the mid-sixties, with the assassination of President Kennedy and the escalating Vietnam War, public unrest and dissatisfaction was mounting. Peaceful demonstrations became violent as the unpopular war divided the country. Inflation and unemployment soared. In 1968, it seemed as though anyone who could think of a reason for it—teachers, garbagemen, nurses, postmen—went out on strike. Racial unrest in many cities, anti-war demonstrations and strikes frazzled the nation's nerves and, for the first time, the Gallup Poll found crime to be our number-one concern. *Life* took stock of the times and summed them up with the complaint "Wherever we look, something's wrong."[60]

At the end of the decade, after the assassinations of Robert Kennedy and Martin Luther King, Jr. that left the country reeling, *Harper's* sent commentator Bill Moyers out on a cross-country trip to feel the nation's pulse. He declared the country "anxious and bewildered.... They don't know what to make of it all."[61] And *Life* took a poll in 1970 that showed that as many as two-thirds of American city dwellers fantasized about escaping to the country.[62]

The crafts revival of the 1960's, which had begun as a reaction against standardization and the dehumanizing factors of technology, gained popularity as the decade of unrest wore on. "Moving to the country" came to stand for making a new start in life, leaving behind a complicated, overheated civilization that nurtured pollution, crime and civil unrest. What had started in Berkeley developed and spread with an evangelist's zeal across the country as skirts and hair grew longer, young women and men resembling their great-grandparents more than their own mothers and fathers. The Age of Aquarius was born. Stewart Brand, the originator of the *Whole Earth Catalog* which first appeared in 1968 and was a staple item in any back-to-earth movement member's backpack, reported to *The New York Times,* "Cities aren't places anymore. They're scenes, projected on screens, then bulldozed away, neighborhood by neighborhood, like cancelled TV shows. . . . Everyone is running for the woods. The drop-out thing has really come to pass. Fear is a lot of it. We have met the enemy and he is us."[63]

A call for a return to the land, escaping the problems and evils of modern life, was accompanied by renewed interest in America's past and the crafts of bygone days. In much the same climate that fostered the Arts and Crafts revival of the late nineteenth century in America, the crafts revival of the 1960's was born. Both revivals were reactions against technology, industrialization and what was regarded as the evils of both. Writing in *The Craftsman* magazine in 1902, Rabbi Joseph Leiser stated, "Air is a luxury in the Ghetto of New York. . . . Millions of our fellow creatures have . . . never breathed fresh air."[64] Sixty-eight years later, a back-to-earth craftsman was quoted in *Life,* "The city puts out too many machine-soot vibrations for me."[65] A belief in the power of individual creativity and the superiority of the handmade over the machine-manufactured object was nurtured by both revivals. And a dread of synthetic, man-made materials accompanied the second resurgence, in which the word "plastic" became synonymous with artificiality, as exemplified by the conversation between a recent college graduate and a glad-handing businessman in the 1967 movie *The Graduate.* Soon, producers of creative, handmade objects in both revivals felt obliged to demand that their work be judged as art, alongside or in place of the more traditionally acceptable paintings and sculptures of their times. This was especially true in the sixties because much of twentieth-century art created since the first Arts and Crafts revival glorified the machine, proclaiming its superiority over the hand of man.

The argument that art or craft should be original rather than a recapitulation of the past was an argument of considerable force in late-nineteenth-century thought and reappeared in the second half of the twentieth century. Late-nineteenth-century schools of painting, most notably the French Impressionists (and their American followers), charted new territory for the traditional arts, the results of which we are still living with today. John Ruskin, a leader of the English Arts and Crafts movement in the 1850's, demanded, "Never encourage imitation or copying of any kind, except for the sake of preserving records of great works."[66] More than a century later and a continent away, an American writing about quiltmaking in 1975 stated, "Whatever you do, do not resort to copying someone else's work....You rob yourself of the experience...of developing your own personal expression."[67]

Revived in both centuries were crafts lost or taken over by machine production. Most notable among these were needlework, furniture making, book design, weaving, stained glass, ceramics, paper making and glass blowing. Writing in 1960, before the advent of the current crafts revival, Reyner Banham lamented the fact that "the precious vessel of handicraft aesthetics that has been passed from hand to hand, was dropped and broken, and no one has bothered to pick up the pieces."[68] Amazingly, twelve short years later, another writer was able to state, "The emphasis on making something with our own hands is one of the central aspects of contemporary design trends."[69] In 1974 a writer rejoiced that "craftsmanship in all endeavors has been reasserted, newly esteemed and made vital. The industrial society's dismissal of the craftsman as a nonconformist, irrelevant eccentric has been laid to rest."[70]

During the 1960's, as more and more of the young and not-so-young moved to the country, they found it difficult to earn more than a subsistence income. Realizing that they needed to supplement that income, these new rural pioneers re-discovered the crafts, like potting, weaving and quiltmaking, which could be done in the home, then sold through co-operatives or in stores. Quilt artist Terrie Hancock Mangat recalls living in the country, warmed by wood fires for which she chopped the logs, making pottery. Some economically depressed areas of the country, sensing opportunity, encouraged people to relocate and start cottage industries making crafts. West Virginia, which was home to several quilting co-operatives, most notably Mountain Artisans and Cabin Creek Quilts,[71] advertised its craft traditions, displaying the works of many new citizens. The state even began a crafts marketing division in 1963 to facilitate its plans, which included organizing fairs and sales events to encourage tourism. One quilt artist, Nancy Crow, remembers seeing quilts for the first time when she visited a West Virginia crafts fair at which Mountain Artisans had a display. By 1977, over two thousand people had taken West Virginia up on its offer and moved there, some buying land for as little as twenty-five dollars an acre.

There were also urban pioneers, most of them young and searching for the same qualities in life as their rural counterparts. Quilt artist Michael James recalls those years when he and his wife lived, as students, in rented apartments. "We were your typical self-helpers," says James. "We did everything ourselves, from baking our own bread to building our own furniture to making all our own clothes."

As the sixties drew to a close, one craft emerged as the overwhelming favorite: quiltmaking. Millions of people have been touched by the quilting revival. Hundreds of books and magazines have been published, thousands of exhibitions held and millions of quilts made. *Quilter's Newsletter Magazine,* regarded by many as the leading magazine for quiltmakers, began in 1969 with a first-issue press run of 5,000 copies. At the end of 1985, it had a paid circulation of over 150,000, with a readership more than double that figure. It is estimated by publishers in the field that over 600,000 people subscribed to at least one quilt magazine in 1986. In 1981, the Oakland (California) Museum mounted a major antique quilt exhibition entitled "American Quilts: A Handmade Legacy." In eighty-one days over 125,000 people paid to see the exhibition, the largest audience that museum has ever recorded. By the mid-1980's, over one thousand quilt guilds and twelve hundred quilt shops were spread across the United States.

As the quilt revival grew during the late sixties and early seventies, leaders in this field were echoing beliefs enunciated by the leaders of the Arts and Crafts movement a century before. In 1966, Jean Ray Laury, regarded by many as the leading voice in the early sixties quilt revival, wrote, "There are no rules in stitchery—no single 'right' way of working."[72] Distancing herself and her audience from kits and patterns, she said, "Stitchery means much the same as needlework, but avoids the connotation of stamped patterns, directions, and limitations."[73] Writing nearly a decade later, another quilt author added, "Ideally, there should be no rigid rules or restrictions connected with creative work."[74] This writer also stressed that "while the basic quilting techniques have remained unchanged for thousands of years, the forms of expression have changed drastically in recent times."[75]

As quilts became more popular, American magazine editors, most of whose offices are within shouting distance of each other in New York City, realized that they were witnessing an event to report, then promote. As quilt artist Michael James reminisces, "The glossy magazines were the only place to see beautifully photographed interiors with quilts. I would faithfully go out looking for those magazines each month, take them home and cut out pictures with quilts in them. I still have file folders filled with those pictures." *Vogue* magazine, long an arbiter of the avant-garde in fashion, was among the first publications in which patchwork began showing up in the 1960's. By the end of the sixties, Diana Vreeland, editor of *Vogue,* had introduced to her international audience the Freedom Quilting Bee, a black, self-help co-operative of quilters in Alabama,[76] and the previously mentioned Mountain Artisans. *House Beautiful, House & Garden* and *Life* joined *Vogue* to give the quilt revival their collective stamp of approval. Month after month, the New York editors turned out story after story about quilts. In October 1968, *Vogue* did a full-color spread on Gloria Vanderbilt's home. Seated in her dressing room, Vanderbilt could be seen with a *Log Cabin* pillow propped up in a chair near her. In December of the same year, *House Beautiful* heralded the revival of patchwork in a pictorial story entitled "Patchwork Quilting: Coming into a Colorful Renascence." It was illustrated with pictures of a patchwork-upholstered couch, along with pillows and a quilt. The interiors in this story were by Parish-Hadley, a well-known interior-design firm which was commissioning works by the Freedom Quilting Bee and Mountain Artisans, helping those quilting co-operatives to land contracts with leading New York City department stores.

In 1969, *Vogue* continued using quilt-inspired fashion within its pages, but in May 1970, a *House Beautiful* columnist prematurely reported the imminent demise of the patchwork craze: "In, but on the way out, the patchwork quilt and the whole patchwork bit."[77] By 1970, advertisers were using patchwork in their ads, and needlepoint kits, acknowledging the quilting revival, began incorporating patchwork-inspired designs and, later, actual quilt patterns. In what even now seems a turning point in the quilt renaissance, Stearns & Foster advertised a quilt pattern in *House Beautiful*: quilting was vying for the attention of the fashion-conscious middle-class woman. Throughout 1970 and 1971, magazines and newspapers were filled with stories about patchwork and quilts.

THE QUILT MOVEMENT was at the right place at the right time. The turbulent 1960's, which had nurtured the back-to-earth movement and fostered the crafts revival, ended with a nation longing for escape from its problems. The prevailing mood was frustration with the present and fear of the future. As one social critic saw it, we had no future except "overpopulation, the bomb and computers eating up our insides."[78] As the seventies began, people reached back to the past and the nostalgia craze began. Old movies and songs, passé clothing styles and early radio programs, folk heroes and handmade crafts soared in popularity. Anything that evoked simpler, safer, less complicated and more innocent times was in demand. *Life* devoted one half of its February 1971 issue to "the sentimental craze for the past"[79] and *Newsweek* evoked the Wizard of Oz by describing nostalgia as "sweeping the country like a Kansas twister."[80] From the 1920's and 1930's came a revival of *No, No, Nanette* and the film version of *The Great Gatsby*. Other movies evoking this earlier time were *The Sting, Paper Moon, Bonnie and Clyde* and *They Shoot Horses, Don't They?* The forties were remembered with Mickey Mouse watches, short shorts (now called hot pants) and the big-band sound. Even the fifties received attention, with Elvis Presley returning in a rhinestone cowboy outfit, and mohawk haircuts and leather jackets becoming the rage; revivalist entertainments like the movie *American Graffiti*, the Broadway musical *Grease* and the television series *Laverne and Shirley* and *Happy Days* were produced.[81]

As people began looking to the past they, like those in the Colonial revival era, began collecting American folk art and antiques. And museums began exhibiting folk art to an ever-widening audience. With growing concern for our way of life, Americans talked animatedly about preserving what was left. Wrote Leopold Tyrmand in *The New Yorker* magazine in August 1969, "I think we have reached the point at which America, having always been prone to rapid change, has to worry more about what to preserve and protect than about what to change....Preserved values and cultural motifs are more powerfully creative than elements of change."[82]

No other craft medium could engender a longing for the past and a feeling of safety in the present like quilts. By the summer of 1971, the New York media establishment was ready for a quilt event, and the Whitney Museum of American Art on Madison Avenue obliged them. Two then-unknown, youthful collectors, Gail van der Hoof and Jonathan Holstein, shared a portion of their burgeoning quilt collection in an exhibition entitled "Abstract Design in American Quilts." It is difficult to overestimate the effect that exhibiting quilts at the Whitney had upon their popularity nationwide. Getting quilts into the Whitney was a curatorial coup. Almost overnight, antique quilts were granted a new, sometimes grudging, respect in the art world. The Whitney exhibition declared them to be objects of art, not "mere" historical objects of interest. As *Quilter's Newsletter Magazine* reported in September 1971, "It seems to be official now — quiltmaking is indeed an art."[83] What was left unsaid was that only antique pieced quilts had been accorded a measured status in the art world.

The critical response to the Whitney exhibition was immediate and overwhelmingly favorable. Hilton Kramer, the august former art editor of *The New York Times*, acknowledging the rarity of such an exhibition cracking the hard shell of established art, wrote, "The Whitney has rarely condescended to acknowledge the 'decorative arts,' as they are called, as a significant contribution to American artistic achievements. One can only hope that the current exhibition, which is of an exceptionally high quality, signals a significant change of heart."[84] Other critics and commentators followed suit. One wrote in *The New Yorker*, "I don't know when an exhibition has given me so much pleasure and so much to think about."[85] David Shapiro, writing in *Craft Horizons*, rhapsodized about the quilts and their "polychrome perfection," declaring them to be "tapestries of courage, stability, intransigence, and intent." To those who would label the quilts as mere women's work, he declared, "Here is a spirit in answer to Rimbaud's almost haughty call for women to be poets. They already were."[86]

Part of the reason that the Whitney exhibition had such a long-lasting effect was that the quilts did not simply remain at the Museum for the exhibition's three-month run, only to be removed, folded and returned to storage. The quilts traveled the nation and Europe for nearly four years, awakening a public and press waiting for official approval of their burgeoning interest in nostalgia. Although the touring exhibition was seen by tens of thousands of people, the residual effect was even greater.

Following the Whitney's lead, magazines showed antique quilts displayed on walls, reminiscent of modern paintings. And museums, in many cases teased into action by the success at the Whitney, began mounting antique-quilt exhibitions.[87] Displaying antique quilts as art had not started at the Whitney, however. In 1965, the Newark (New Jersey) Museum, at the height of the Op Art craze, mounted "Optical Quilts." In reviewing the exhibition, *Time* called it "Op art from prior centuries."[88] *Newsweek* reviewed an Op Art exhibition at New York's Museum of Modern Art, referring back to the Newark quilts, calling them some of the liveliest Op Art pieces on view.[89] Because of the "Optical Quilts" exhibition, quilts were, for the first time, viewed primarily for their aesthetic beauty rather than their historical interest or technical achievements. Critics, many unaware until now of the sophisticated geometric patterning in old quilts and scrambling to cover their tracks, announced that the quilts were stark, bold statements of artistic merit. Jean Ray Laury wrote in 1970, with seeming tongue-in-cheek understatement, "The 'optical' and 'pop' art forms of today are often found in early American quilts and are being newly appreciated."[90] By 1973, modern art galleries far from the borders of Manhattan were displaying antique quilts where Stellas or Vasarélys had been hanging just days before. The John Berggruen Gallery in San Francisco and the James Corcoran Gallery in Los Angeles were among the galleries to join in the quilt renaissance. In 1974, a writer in *Art News* reported that in one month of that year there were ten museums highlighting quilt exhibitions.

After viewing quilts in magazines or exhibitions, Americans by the thousands began buying them and the antiques business reeled as it watched young dealers, most of them entirely new to the business, buying quilts with abandon, quilts that two years earlier would have been used to protect furniture from scratches and dents, then turning and selling the same quilts for quick profits to euphoric collectors. By the end of the 1970's, almost every major American city had at least one successful quilt dealer, specializing in not much more than the quilted bedcoverings of the past. The hills and valleys of New England, Pennsylvania, New York, Ohio, Indiana, Maryland and Virginia were alive with dealers going door to door, auction to auction, bidding up the prices of quilts. The action, though less fierce, was nonetheless taking place across the country. Early New York

City dealers laid their selections out on tables, offering to let interested collectors take their pick for twenty-five dollars. By the mid-seventies, however, prices had mushroomed and the late seventies and eighties would see the prices of quilts skyrocket as the supply from country towns and farms dwindled under the crushing weight of unbridled demand. This mercantile activity further fueled the interests of editors and writers who rushed to interview dealers and collectors. The activity led well-known quilt dealer Roderick Kiracofe to comment, "If there's anybody out there who doesn't know about quilts by now, they must be living on a remote island." Indeed, the interest in quilts seemed all-consuming. Quilt artist Pauline Burbidge remembers the early seventies in London, England, where the interest in antique quilts was also rising. "I had an antiques stall on the Portobello Road in London. Well, a table actually. And I sold second-hand things. I was going around to jumble sales and buying old clothes and things. That's where I first saw old quilts. Then, I came across Ruth Finley's book. Having that book just started me off. After that, I got Ruby McKim's book and did a butterfly quilt from her pattern. It was my first quilt and I worked out the techniques on my own. After doing that quilt I wanted to be a quiltmaker." Quilt artists Nancy Crow and Michael James have both mentioned the influence of antique quilts on their work and both have singled out the quilts of Amish seamstresses in particular. Quilt dealers and, as a consequence, magazine editors were quick to tout the richly colored Amish quilts in simple geometric designs. Even more than other old quilts, Amish ones could most easily be defined by their visual association with modern painting. Being thus easy to categorize and label in ways familiar to a modern audience, Amish quilts grew in popularity and climbed in price dramatically. Says Michael James, "The idea that quilts can be art may not have occurred to me had I not seen Amish quilts."

As the interest in quilts threatened to become a national phenomenon, Americans were facing harder economic times. Inflation, an insignificant factor in the average American's plans for the future during the 1960's, became the number-one topic of discussion. Prices for necessities like bread reached heights few Americans had ever considered possible. People began stockpiling staple items, fearing that prices might outstrip their pocketbooks. When gasoline prices jumped threefold, Americans waited in lines that stretched for blocks in order to top up their gas tanks, fearing that they might be unable to get to work. As if all these new economic facts of life were not enough to struggle with, unemployment rose at rates that brought to mind the Great Depression. With high gas prices keeping people at home and increased leisure time caused by a shrinking job market, crafts became the answer to what to do with very little money and a lot of unexpected free time. People started making objects to brighten their homes or to give as gifts, stretching the value of their dollars.

In fact, quiltmaking more than any other craft benefited from the economic slump. Hundreds of thousands of women took up the craft, most for the first time. And many of these women discovered that they could supplement their incomes by doing something they enjoyed. A late 1973 headline in *The New York Times* read, "Mothers with Crafts on their Hands Find a Place to Sell Them." The article chronicled the emergence of shops taking crafts for sale on consignment. Quilt shops were among those which did. Quilt artists Terrie Hancock Mangat, Pamela Studstill and Nancy Crow remember supplementing their incomes during this period with crafts they had made. Mangat sold handmade buttons and pottery at fairs, Studstill ran a handmade clothing store with a friend and Crow sold leather handbags to finance her quiltmaking. Sensing there was money to be made from this crafts revival that refused to die, department stores opened sales areas devoted exclusively to handmade items. New York's fashionable Bergdorf Goodman replaced a sluggish shoe department with a handicraft boutique and Macy's staged a week-long crafts fair to promote needlework kits.[91] Quilt artist Risë Nagin sold silk-screened baby clothes to Bergdorf Goodman and Saks Fifth Avenue. Several large stores also sold craft supplies. In fact, the boom was so great that between 1965 and 1974 sales of hobby supplies doubled.[92] Businesses selling raw materials for crafts or publishing how-to books found profits up for the first time in years. During 1969–1970, *McCall's Needlework and Crafts* magazine was forced to print five-hundred thousand more copies than it had planned.[93] Said one bemused editor of crafts books who noticed how the middle class and back-to-earth advocates had joined one another in making crafts, "Everyone is working with their hands and for diametrically opposed political reasons."[94]

With galloping inflation making traditional investments at low interest rates less attractive, many Americans with money to spare started buying art and antiques. Business at America's auction houses and

A photograph from the February 1973 issue of House & Garden. With an abandon that would make any serious collector wince, House & Garden covered even the floors with antique quilts, stating, "Quilts have jumped off the bed to blaze across walls and floors, sofas, pillows, even tables, to show they are a decorative art in every room in the house." Photograph courtesy of House & Garden. Copyright © 1973 The Condé Nast Publications, Inc.

among art and antiques dealers soared, and prices kept pace. Antique quilts sold fast and for increasingly larger prices. Knowing that the "country look" was popular among the well-heeled and would continue to grow with a little coaxing, America's editors flooded the newsstands with cover articles on decorating with country antiques and folk art, planting country flower and vegetable gardens, and canning, baking bread and quiltmaking. In fact, the canning craze got so heated at one point that there was a national shortage of canning-jar rings. By 1972, *House & Garden* was devoting a four-page spread to the "Craft Comeback, Folk Art, Decorative Inspiration: The All-American Patchwork Quilt." In the text that accompanied the full-color photographs, the writer explained, "In pioneer days quilts were always used as bedcovers, made solely for warmth and comfort. Today they are cropping up everywhere. Not simply rolled up at the end of the bed, quilts are now hung, draped, stuffed, and folded — and they are being imitated in fabric and paint, and in the 'patchwork put-together' of whole room schemes."[95] To accommodate its readers' interest in the art of quiltmaking, *House & Garden* recommended, "For private lessons: [Beth] Gutcheon, . . . who teaches during the day at New York University, will give evening instruction by appointment. In California, Jean Ray Laury gives quiltmaking lessons."[96] Laury and Gutcheon were staunch advocates of creative experimentation as the quilt revival gained momentum. By 1974, manufacturers were awake to the quilt revival as patchwork-inspired prints could be found on bedspreads, curtains, pillows, tablecloths, clothes, jigsaw puzzles, wallpapers, carpets, dishes, napkins, placemats, wrapping paper, sheets and upholstery fabric. Like a self-fulfilling prophecy, the quilt revival forged ahead, powered now by its own momentum. The press could not get its fill of the subject. Quilt artist Jean Hewes remembers she was so influenced by the stories appearing in newspapers and magazines that she made her first quilt after having read an article in the *Chicago Tribune*.

With thousands of American women interested in making quilts for the first time, more quilt shops began appearing across the country and quilt guilds formed, some swelling to memberships of several hundred. By 1973, *Quilter's Newsletter Magazine* was advertising for new subscribers in upscale *House & Garden*. As more and more people became interested in making crafts, the number of courses offered by schools and community centers proliferated. Although most of these new students were motivated by an interest in learning a skill, some took classes for blatantly mercantile reasons. Re-marked one crafts-shop owner, "A man came into my shop the other day and said, 'Would you be interested in buying jewelry?' I said, 'Sure, what do you make?' He said, 'Well, nothing right now. I'm taking a course at junior college.' I said, 'Well, what's your teach-er's name?' 'I don't know,' he answered, 'I missed the first part of the course.' "[97] As if the press's incessant coverage were not enough to encourage would-be quiltmakers to take up their needles, along came the Bicentennial celebration to spark their interest. In 1976, as the nation celebrated the Bicentennial, *Good Housekeeping* announced a national quilt contest. Quilts made from kits were ineligible, the em-phasis thus falling upon creative stitchery. Among the nearly 10,000 entrants was quilt artist Terrie Hancock Mangat, who was a regional winner. The volume of entries was staggering: the magazine's staff had estimated that 3,500 quilts would be completed for the contest.[98]

As the renewed interest in quilts grew, it was inevitable that prod-ucts requiring scant creativity would return to the marketplace, just as they had in the 1930's. Kits and project-oriented how-to books are easy to market to an indulgent new audience, hungry for infor-mation and help. And businesses, sensing there was money to be made, entered the field in droves. Soon the marketplace was filled with simple-minded patchwork projects that took little skill and no imagination.

But the call for creativity was not silenced. Many fine, juried tradi-tional quilt exhibitions were held. In addition, exhibitions began ap-pearing in which a new type of quilt was shown, one markedly different from its tradition-inspired counterparts. One of the first such exhibitions was "The New American Quilt" at The Museum of Contemporary Crafts in New York City in 1976. Quilt artists Gayle Fraas and Duncan Slade were participants. Since experimentation for its own sake was popular in the arts at this time, many of the quilts selected for "The New American Quilt," typical of many early contemporary quilts, displayed techniques, styles, forms and subject matter which were in formative stages of development. Many of the early contemporary quilts were also greatly influenced by, and faint echoes of, the Pop Art movement which had gained the status of a cause célèbre. But the fact remained that the more established and recognized crafts world, which until now had snubbed quiltmaking, was taking another look at this startlingly popular medium.[99] In 1979, due in part to the energy and leadership of quilt artist Nancy Crow,

"Quilt National" was born. Sponsored by the Southeastern Ohio Cultural Arts Center, this biennial juried exhibition was the first to spotlight contemporary, often original, designs instead of traditional ones. Crow was a member of a small quilting group in southeast Ohio whose members felt isolated from fellow contemporary quilt-makers around the country. Creating contemporary designs them-selves, they wanted to see what other quiltmakers were attempting. Four years after the first "Quilt National" came the controversial "The Artist & The Quilt" in 1983, a traveling exhibition for which eighteen women artists were asked to create designs which were then translated to the quilt medium by quiltmakers; in some in-stances, the artist worked closely with the quiltmaker. However, feeling that the participating needleworkers were relegated to sub-servient roles by this approach, many traditional quiltmakers and contemporary quilt artists resented the apparent slap at the creative abilities of all quilters.[100] Regardless of the criticisms leveled at it by its detractors, "The Artist & The Quilt" was yet another proof that the art world, long resistant to recognizing the fabric arts, would eventually be forced to surrender to the intrinsic artistic merit of the quilt medium.

AS AMERICA CHANGED dramatically after World War II, so did the art world. By the mid-fifties, Pop Art was changing the way artists commented upon their environ-ment. No longer was art confined to being a reflection of artists struggling intellectually to define their worlds. Now, everyday, often technological or commercial, objects domi-nated their art. Popular culture—comic strips, advertising and mer-chandise—was touted as acceptable subject matter by artists who wished to tease and expand the boundaries of what they considered to be a too-traditional, backward-looking definition of art. Just as, for generations, quiltmakers have used common objects from the real world as symbols in their creations, so now did modern artists. In fact, it seemed that the more common the object, the greater the artists' enthusiasm for it. And, as in quiltmaking, Pop Artists often flattened these common symbols for the two-dimensional plane, repeating them in a grid pattern reminiscent of quilt block forma-tions used in much of traditional quilt construction.

Not only were artists adding to the list of acceptable subject matter, they were also experimenting with materials not normally associated with the "fine arts." It was not long before collage assemblages, incorporating paper and cloth, reminiscent of early twentieth-century works by Braque, Picasso, Ernst and Dove, began reappearing. Artists like Claes Oldenburg, Christo, George Segal and, later, Alan Shields began using fabric in a wide variety of ways, exploiting the versatility of cloth to be torn, cut, folded, draped, dyed, painted, burned, sewn and stuffed. In 1963, Oldenburg was creating "soft sculptures," piecing canvas cloth together on a machine with the aid of his wife, then stuffing the forms with foam rubber. By painting the forms to resemble hamburgers, typewriters and even cake slices, Oldenburg transformed subject matter that was considered "low" into "high art." Though controversial, his work was embraced by museums, critics and collectors. And along with other early Pop Artists like Roy Lichtenstein, Andy Warhol, Jasper Johns and James Rosenquist, he changed the direction of twentieth-century art.

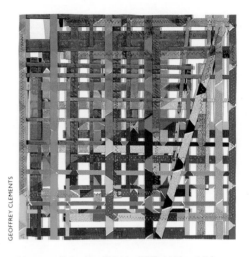

Newport II, *by Alan Shields, 1973, 14¼ × 14¼ inches, silkscreen, flocking and thread on paper. One side of a two-sided work. Edition of twelve. Photograph courtesy of Paula Cooper Gallery, New York City.*

Christo began wrapping objects in fabric as early as 1958. By the late sixties he was using fabric to wrap everything from the Museum of Contemporary Art in Chicago to part of the Australian coastline.[101] Using fabric as his primary means of expression in his monumental works, Christo was making a statement that was not lost on his contemporaries. Likewise, sculptor George Segal chose plaster-soaked fabric for his life-size human figures. Painter Alan Shields, who was taught to sew with a machine by his mother and two sisters (he owns twenty sewing machines), started to sew fabric pieces together in making his paintings. He first discovered that machine-stitched lines made a beautiful pattern on his canvases when he was sewing a binding on a painting's edge to keep the canvas from stretching. Says Shields, "When you put two lines of machine stitching together it is very special because they are not continuous lines, there is electricity because of the dot and dash pattern."[102]

As fabric was used extensively by established artists, younger ones beginning their careers rarely questioned its acceptability. As artist Anne Healy states, "Cloth is something we all relate to from birth to death. It is associated with every event of our lives. . . . It's a magical medium which is itself and yet appears to be so many other things."[103] And artists utilizing other materials began imitating the properties of fabric—its softness and pliability—in their work. Lynda Benglis, working in copper, created a series of wall sculptures in which the metal was transformed to look like knotted fabric.

Bed, by Robert Rauschenberg, 1955,
75¼ × 31½ × 6½ inches, "combine
painting" on wood supports, with oil and
pencil on pillow, quilt and sheet. Collection of
Mr. and Mrs. Leo Castelli.

Fan Dance, by Barton Beneš, 1981, 56 × 38
inches, mixed media. Photograph courtesy of
Hokin/Kaufman Gallery, Chicago.

As the list of acceptable subject matter lengthened, artists began taking seemingly unrelated materials and media and re-assembling them to form a new whole. Early on, Robert Rauschenberg's *Bed* (this page) and Ann Wilson's *Moby Dick,* both painted in 1955, incorporated *Log Cabin* quilts.[104] And artists intent on experimentation have continued this additive approach to creating art into the present day. Mixed-media specialist Barton Beneš created a series of collages in 1981 based upon a *Fan* quilt made by his aunt's grandmother (this page).[105] This approach of taking bits and pieces and putting them together to create an entirely new image is identical in spirit to that employed by quiltmakers. It is not surprising, therefore, that artists were more and more influenced by quilts as they experimented. As the mid-seventies approached, a group of artists known as pattern painters emerged. They were interested in designs and patterns found in functional decorative art objects like quilts, tapestries, needlework, baskets, carpets, wallpaper and mosaic tiles. The pattern, instead of the object, became the subject of their art. The leading exponent of this new movement was Miriam Schapiro, whose work continues to be influenced by the precepts of pattern painting.[106] Her *Wonderland* (facing page), completed in 1983, is but one example.

At the same time that artists were becoming more and more interested in what had once been considered everyday household objects, the feminist movement was gaining strength. This movement, which formed, among diverse goals, to secure equal political and economic rights for women, also fostered a deep, abiding interest in the traditional female crafts. Quiltmaking, because it was already enjoying a renaissance, became a very popular subject and quilts, for many women, became flags around which to rally. Feminist artists like Schapiro began incorporating more and more female images in their works and quilt images predominated in many. Artist Sondra Freckelton has included quilts in many of her works (facing page). Not only is she enthusiastic about the rhythmic tempo found in quilt patterns, utilizing them to move the eye of the viewer around a painting, but she feels quilts "are our visual history. . . . They don't speak about wars and kings, but about life—about how we slept and ate and dreamed and lived."[107] As women artists gained the respect of the male-dominated art profession, images associated with women, like quilts, began showing up in more and more art works made by men. And as women studied their artifacts, they became interested in the female ancestors who had created them. This feminist interest in, for example, nineteenth-century quiltmakers fueled much of the valuable research in quilt history completed during the 1970's and 1980's. Among feminist artists, this interest was also readily apparent. For example, Linda Plotkin's *Ancestors* (next page) needs no written interpretation. As female artists have increased in stature and number, they have continued to include images from female artifacts in their works. Miriam Schapiro's *Autobiography* (next page), resembling a traditional Sampler quilt, is a rich example of such influences. Male artists have also been interested in their ancestors who quilted. Artist David Schirm remembered his quiltmaking grandmother in a painting (page 57). Schirm says that she "made her quilts in her bedroom which was so small that the quilting frame formed a low canopy over her bed.... When she was ill she would sit in bed like Matisse and sew on the designs."[108] Other male artists have been influenced by living relatives who quilt. The artist's quiltmaking wife sleeps in David Bates' *The Dream* (page 57) and James Valerio used *Ruth and Cecil Him* (page 58) to demonstrate his close association with quiltmaking. The Hims are friends made because of his wife's membership in a local quilt guild.

As the hard line separating "craft" from "art" has blurred, artists have started creating works which resemble, but are not meant to be used as, functional, everyday objects. Margaret Wharton's *Heirloom* (page 58) and Jane Kaufman's untitled crazy quilt (page 59) are

Still Life, by Sondra Freckelton, 1978–1979, 60 × 40 inches, watercolor on paper. Collection of The Owens-Corning Collection, Owens-Corning Fiberglas Corporation, Toledo, Ohio.

Wonderland, by Miriam Schapiro, 1983, 90 × 144 inches, acrylic paint and fabric on canvas. Photograph courtesy of the artist. Courtesy of Bernice Steinbaum Gallery, New York City.

Ancestors, by Linda Plotkin, 1983, 48 × 66 inches, oil on canvas. Photograph courtesy of G. W. Einstein Company, Inc., New York City.

but two examples of this trend. Demonstrating the potential for change within the art establishment, Kaufman's work was hung by a prominent New York City gallery in 1985 without exhaustive explanation.[109]

Given the movement of artists toward experimentation with materials and media, and the resultant inclusion of fabric and quilt images in "mainstream" art, it is not surprising that a group of serious quilt artists has emerged. Regrettably, these artists face considerable resistance from the male-dominated art establishment which, for the most part, continues to associate fabric with "women's work." This denial of the changing role of fabric in art is spurious, especially in light of the growing interaction among the media. However, the denial verges on the ludicrous when trained painters, printmakers, watercolorists and other artists give up their canvases and paper to work in cloth and thread, only to find the world of art suddenly closed to them. Indeed, it makes no sense, given the historical perspective, for trained, experienced artists working creatively within the quilt medium to be barred from the art world.

Autobiography, by Miriam Schapiro, 1982, 60 × 50 inches, acrylic paint and fabric on canvas. Photograph courtesy of the artist. Courtesy of Bernice Steinbaum Gallery, New York City.

THE ANTIQUE QUILT exhibitions of the 1960's and 1970's did more than re-awaken interest in America's quilted bedcoverings. These exhibitions moved quilts from beds and the horizontal plane to walls and the vertical. And because many of the quilts exhibited were patterned in intricate, boldly colored geometrics akin to twentieth-century art, the modern art audience could not resist the temptation to label these antique creations as startling precursors of modern art, worthy of their newly acquired positions in the art world.

Now that the quilt had made the official leap from bed to wall,[110] thousands of contemporary quiltmakers needed no further stimulus. As previously stated, by the mid-seventies they were making quilts specifically for wall display, never intending that their creations would grace a four-poster. Even traditionally crafted new quilts were exhibited on walls instead of the beds for which they were intended. Of course, there were those who protested that the walls were reserved for antique quilts, clinging to the intellectually indefensible position that "old" was easily translatable to "art" while "new" denoted "mere craft." The leading advocates of such tripe were, of course, often the people with the most to gain economically from such arguments—the antique quilt dealers and collectors. But their protestations were usually heard only by those in related fields who

The Dream, by David Bates, 1983, 90 × 72 inches, oil on canvas. Private collection. Photograph courtesy of Charles Cowles Gallery, New York City.

While Working on Her Patchwork Quilts, Nana Thought She Had a Vision, But When She Turned Her Head To Look, It Wasn't There, by David Schirm, 1983, 22 × 30 inches, mixed media on paper. Photograph courtesy of the artist.

Ruth and Cecil Him, by James Valerio, 1982,
92¼ × 80¼ inches, oil on canvas. Collection
of Dr. Robert Shimshak. Photograph courtesy
of Allan Frumkin Gallery, New York City.

Heirloom, by Margaret Wharton, 1985,
54 × 17½ × 30 inches, mixed media,
including wood, cloth and epoxy. Photograph
courtesy of Phyllis Kind Gallery, Chicago.

feared they, too, might be outnumbered by enthusiastic hordes of contemporary practitioners. To those for whom scarcity of number was an economic fortress, the spectre of hundreds of thousands of avid quiltmakers turning out millions of quilts a year resembled a siege. Not surprisingly, what is often forgotten by advocates of an art form was forgotten in this case: that only some examples within any art form truly deserve the status of "art." Therefore, contrary to how their admirers were categorizing antique and modern quilts en masse, only a portion of the quilts in either category were worthy of the argument, a point lost on virtually all of the debaters.

Within the quiltmaking movement, controversies were also arising. The established tradition of quiltmaking allows for self-expression within a set, mutually agreed-upon format. One can bend the rules but is expected not to break them. The format for pieced quilts (and, to a lesser extent, appliqués) allows for design and color modifications and, occasionally, design originality. Traditional piecing is copy work with adaptation. Since the overwhelming majority of pieced quilts are geometrics, a quiltmaker is already working within set bounds. (Traditional geometric quilt patterns were, of course, originally created, but *then* they are copied and adapted by all who use them.) Much can be accomplished within these mutually accepted limitations; if, however, some quiltmakers want to modify the rules, changing, expanding or even destroying the original intent, the tranquility derived from an ordered system is jarred. This is what happened as budding young quilt artists began experimenting with the quilt medium. The natural reaction of those who were happy with the traditionally ordered system was to resist, and a tension developed between the traditional and contemporary practitioners of modern quiltmaking. Such tensions are common in any endeavor; change is never an easy companion of tradition. Indeed, throughout quiltmaking history there are examples of such tensions. Up to the present, the most obvious of these occurred in the second half of the nineteenth century, as fancy silk work supplanted the long-practiced tradition of sewing with calico. As the *Crazy* came into vogue, it stretched the very definition of a quilt.[111] Its construction was similar to that used in making a *Log Cabin*,[112] another quilt style that had expanded the quiltmaker's vocabulary earlier in the century. The *Crazy*'s practitioners, however, moved beyond merely experimenting with construction and brought new techniques and materials to the art of quiltmaking. These included ornate embroidery and embellishments — beads, metallic threads, paintings, photographs, three-dimensional flowers and even taxidermically stuffed animals[113] — the likes of which had never appeared on quilts before. This fashion of decorating the surfaces of crazy quilts was, in part, a reaction against the tenets of traditional quiltmaking, and its development and demise are similar in part to that of the pattern-painting movement of the 1970's. Just as pattern painting's achievements have been absorbed by the art world and, as a movement, pattern painting is no longer a viable entity, the technical and stylistic advances achieved in crazy quilts were synthesized by the quiltmaking system, and the Victorian silk works themselves slowly disappeared.

Today's quilt artists are keenly aware that their experimentations with format, color, techniques and subject matter have been met by resistance from some traditional quiltmakers, but quilt artist Yvonne Porcella echoes the feelings of her associates when she states, "I hope there won't be a division between traditional quiltmakers and quilt artists. I hope we can work side by side and respect and admire and learn from each other's work." Porcella continues, "I feel a strong link to earlier quiltmakers. And I feel a strong link to today's traditional quiltmakers as well. We came to quiltmaking for basically the same reasons." Quilt artist Joan Schulze concurs, saying, "Quiltmaking is an important means of expression for whoever makes a quilt, whether you call yourself an artist or not." Terrie Hancock Mangat goes even further: "I still enjoy making a traditional quilt. It's fun. And remember: there may be boring traditional quilts, but there are also boring contemporary ones, as well as boring art in every medium."

The tension between the traditional and the avant-garde will continue in quiltmaking, just as it does in all meaningful forms of human expression. What is important is perspective. One hundred years ago, as makers of elaborate crazy quilts experimented beyond the bounds of the calico-quilt tradition, never could they have guessed that today a quilt artist like Terrie Hancock Mangat would be including both traditional piecework *and* elaborate embellishment in all her works. For all of today's quiltmakers, the past century's controversies are mere footnotes in the story of the quilt's steady development as a medium of artistic expression. The controversies of today may seem just as irrelevant fifty years from now.

Indeed, the quilt artists shown here could be regarded as strict traditionalists, if only their quiltmaking techniques were catalogued. The bold embellishments found on works like Mangat's have their

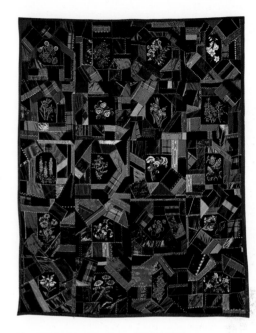

Untitled, by Jane Kaufman, 1983–1985, 94 × 82 inches, crazy quilt with beads and embroidery. Photograph courtesy of Bernice Steinbaum Gallery, New York City.

counterparts in Victorian silk work, as already mentioned. The color photocopy work that quilt artist Joan Schulze uses in many of her quilts is grounded in the late-nineteenth-century tradition of transferring photographic images to cloth so that they can be included in a prized quilt, often an autobiographical statement similar in intent to Schulze's *Self-Portrait* (plate 17). Embroidery, which is seen in works by Mangat, has existed in America's bedcoverings since the early crewel works of the eighteenth century. Painting on quilts, a technique employed by several of the quilt artists, developed in the latter half of the nineteenth century. Stenciling (or stamping), used by quilt artist Deborah Felix, appeared on America's bedcoverings by the early nineteenth century, and dyeing cloth to achieve an otherwise unavailable color, as exemplified by quilt artist Jan Myers-Newbury is as old as quiltmaking itself.

The difference, then, between the works of these quilt artists and more traditional quilts is not in techniques, but in the application of those techniques and in the choice of subject matter. For no quiltmaker can argue with the technical expertise displayed in the piecing by Pauline Burbidge and Pamela Studstill or the ability to manipulate color possessed by Michael James and Nancy Crow, just as none can question the innovative embroidery of Terrie Hancock Mangat or the dye knowledge of Gayle Fraas, Duncan Slade and Jan Myers-Newbury. Today's quilt artists are proficient in the technical aspects of their craft and, being so, they are applying those techniques in new ways as they expand beyond the subject matter once considered appropriate for quilts.

Although geometric patterning and flora are areas of interest for many of the quilt artists, others in the group are not restricting their creativity to these traditional forms alone. One need only look at the mixed-media creations of Terrie Hancock Mangat and Therese May, the composite works of Jean Hewes, the iconographic images of Joan Schulze, the purposely satirical, art historical judgments of Deborah Felix and the architectural constructions of Gayle Fraas and Duncan Slade to realize that these artist are exploring subjects their predecessors a mere generation ago could not have imagined.

An art form possesses an ordered structure that includes an accepted, though often contested, definition of the medium. "What is a quilt?" is a question heard with greater frequency as quilt artists experiment on the outer borders of the medium and traditionalists, working nearer the center, watch to see which of the once-unquestioned tenets is disputed next. Using the tradition-bound definition of a quilt, one can argue that some of the works exhibited here are not quilts. Interestingly, individual viewers may select different quilts to demonstrate their particular prejudices, feeling that the quilts denounced by someone else are perfectly acceptable. To be certain, anyone who knows the medium will harbor prejudices against experimentation as it nears any of one's favored precepts. Yet this strict definition of a quilt might, if applied to antique quilts or some traditionally made modern ones, also eliminate long-accepted examples of, or adjuncts to, the medium.

The quilt, as a creative form of expression, is constantly being re-evaluated by its creators. It is important to remember that, most often, it is the commentators *on* a creative art form, not the creators *of* it, who question experimentation and are frightened by it. The creators know that all quiltmakers, for example, are constantly experimenting, some within the defined tenets of the art, some outside. It is through change that anything of merit evolves. That is not to say that all change or experimentation is valid. We need only look to the past 150 years of quiltmaking to see the scattered carcasses of once-adulated trends and gimmicks. But without experimentation and change, without creative pioneers who are willing to test the limits of any art form, that art form will surely die, if from nothing more than the sheer weight of its own tedium.

By the next generation, art colleges ought to be offering degrees in quiltmaking. However, the quilt artists shown here received their training in other media before selecting the quilt as their mode of expression. Fourteen of these eighteen quilt artists hold M.F.A., B.F.A. or M.A. degrees in such varied areas as painting, watercolor, printmaking, ceramics, design, fashion and textiles. Up until very recently, the world of quiltmaking was a necessarily insular one, its practitioners learning from each other and innovations coming from within the community of needlewomen.[114] It was not until the feminist movement began in the early 1970's, and more and more women challenged the male-dominated art establishment, that quiltmaking caught the interest of women (and men) who possessed professional art backgrounds. Today, there are many quilt artists, including the ones shown here, who are working in the medium. They bring to it a broad repertoire of artistic talents. As a result, they have, through the use of these talents, expanded the format, scale and subject matter of quilts. Before them, quiltmaking was, for the most part dependent upon a catalogue of established geometric and appliqué patterns. Now, however, trained artists are making one original design after another and, as is the case with several of them, they are manipulating the traditional geometric plane with a new vivacity. In turn, their work has challenged tens of thousands of contemporary *and* traditional quiltmakers, the overwhelming majority without academic art backgrounds, to experiment with color and pattern, to innovate. As thousands of quiltmakers who might otherwise consider themselves traditionalists have studied with quilt artists like Burbidge, Crow, James, Myers-Newbury and Porcella, they have translated what they have learned to their own quilts. The laudatory results have helped rescue modern quiltmaking from the mass-produced patchwork projects that proliferated during the seventies and eighties. Thus, the influence of these quilt artists goes far beyond their own artistic output; it includes their powerful influence on the whole of modern quiltmaking.

To an observer of the arts, a switch from an accepted medium like painting, watercolor or ceramics[115] to an uncertain future in quiltmaking is tantamount to professional suicide. If you are creating work that no museum and few galleries will show, how do you become recognized, able to sell your work so that you can afford to continue making it? This is, of course, a question as old as the arts themselves, but it is a particularly nagging one for quilt artists who have had their works rejected, as "acceptable" media have openly borrowed subjects and techniques from quiltmaking. Several of the artists have pursued teaching and the occasional commission or been supported by an understanding spouse or friend. And some, like many of their fellow craftsmen and artists, have "taken to the hills," living simply, pursuing their art in rural settings rather than more expensive cities. "We spent our first two years in the country," reminisce Gayle Fraas and Duncan Slade, who continue to live in a rural setting, "using what can only be described as a primitive dye technology for our work: we had a hand pump and a watering can. There wasn't even running water."

The decision to commit themselves to quiltmaking, in the face of enormous odds, seems, however, to have been a choice most of these artists made with anticipation as they discovered the quilt's potential for artistic expression. They were drawn, as are all true artists, by their medium, not by its remunerative benefits or its acceptability. Displaying a tenacity prevalent in the group, quilt artist

Deborah Felix reports that "painters ask me why I don't paint. I like to give Nancy Crow's response to this: she asks them why they don't make quilts." And, although it will not surprise fellow quiltmakers, it is the appeal of fabric that joins these artists in their pursuit of quiltmaking. Seven of the artists have sewn since childhood. They were already aware of some of the advantages—and disadvantages—fabric has over other materials. As a result, the medium was a natural one for them. "I've always collected fabric," says quilt artist Terrie Hancock Mangat. "When I was six years old, my mom asked me what I wanted for Christmas. I said 'fabric.' She bought me six one-half-yard pieces and wrapped them up. They meant so much to me; I kept them in a box and took them out to enjoy them. However, it wasn't until I'd graduated from art college that I realized I could use fabric in my art instead of the 'approved' media." Others in the group have strong memories of grandmothers and mothers who made quilts or, as is the case with Gayle Fraas and Duncan Slade, mothers who were seamstresses. These quilt artists could anticipate the medium's pleasures, having watched their mothers or grandmothers sewing. Yet for the trained artist whose teachers never mentioned quiltmaking as a professional alternative, the choice of quilts was not an obvious one. For Jan Myers-Newbury, who has sewn since she was six and been influenced by two quiltmaking grandmothers, "It never occurred to me that I could use my sewing for my art." Having struggle for years to find a medium that felt good to her, she "re-discovered" quiltmaking after pursuing an M.A. in design.

Quilt artist Joan Schulze, echoing the sentiments of the group, was immediately drawn to the medium's tactile qualities. Says Schulze, "The more you handle fabric, the more it tells you what to do." Adds Nancy Crow, "Paint just doesn't interest me the way fabric does. I like to touch fabric, to slide my fingers into its folds." Risë Nagin, whose shimmering works are crafted from a variety of fabrics from around the world, is also drawn by the medium's tactile appeal. She enjoys working with fabric for its "sensuality," and adds, "I also like the way it catches the light; it's very different from paint." Quilt artist Pauline Burbidge, who worked with fabric as a fashion major in art college, shares this appreciation for the tactile sensitivities of cloth, but it was the construction process inherent in quiltmaking that attracted her most strongly. "I remember my first quilt," Burbidge says. "The piecing was like therapy." Michael James shares this deep attraction to piecing, describing it as a "building process." Says James, "It's a

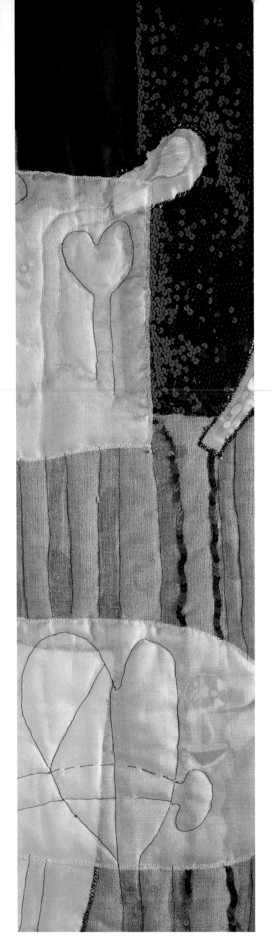

lot like designing silkscreening, which was one of my major concentrations before turning to quiltmaking."

Quilt artists Jean Hewes, Nancy Crow, Yvonne Porcella, Joan Schulze and Therese May were young mothers when they began quiltmaking in earnest. May, who was a painter, and Hewes, who had created large ceramics similar in feeling to the figures in her current works, found they could not pursue these media with small children demanding their attentions. Quiltmaking, on the other hand, could be picked up and worked on, as time permitted, inside or outside the home. Crow, Porcella and Schulze found they could, like so many of their fellow quiltmakers, run a home and still have some time for their artistry. Quilt artist Ruth McDowell does so today.

Hewes, who was also trained as a watercolorist, found she was attracted to the transparent nature of fabric. Her works, with their recurrent use of gauzes and other lightweight fabrics (this page), are illustrative of how one quilt artist has adapted her previous training to the medium of quiltmaking. Adds Hewes, "Neither watercolor nor ceramics were as complicated to me as is quiltmaking." Likewise, with extraordinary finesse, Pamela Studstill, who still works as a painter, adds her own patterns to fabric with paint, combining this talent with her interest in the intricacies of piecework (facing page, top). "I've always been interested in the color theories of the Impressionists and the fact that when you put two small bits of color side by side the eye mixes them," says Studstill. "By painting on my fabrics, I achieve a greater range of color and pattern than would be possible by using just solid-colored fabrics." Therese May, more than any of the other trained painters in the group, combines fabric and paint in the style of many mixed-media specialists and pattern painters (page 66, top). Joan Schulze, echoing the growing sentiment within the group, says, "Quiltmaking gives me the chance to use all the techniques I know."

The quilt artists shown here began their quiltmaking as early as 1966 and as late as 1977, with most of them starting in the early 1970's. Two of the early leaders in the movement, Michael James and Nancy Crow, continue to work within the geometric plane, finding new ways to manipulate its infinite possibilities. They, like pieced-quilt specialists Pauline Burbidge and Ruth McDowell, have restricted their materials to those most closely associated with traditionally pieced quilts, although James and Burbidge have used silks in works shown here and McDowell almost exclusively uses cotton blends

Detail from plate 21.

and synthetic fabrics. These quiltmakers, like Studstill, Myers and Porcella, are re-defining the geometric pieced quilt.

It is interesting that painters learned to incorporate fabric into their canvases, adding new dimension and texture to their works, just as quilt artists are now applying bits of canvas to their quilts. Terrie Hancock Mangat has used not only painted canvas as an embellishment on her quilts, but also elaborate embroidery (right) and a wide variety of three-dimensional forms (page 67, bottom). Like Hewes, who often includes sequins (facing page) and embroidery in her pieces, Mangat has turned the tables on the pattern painters of the 1970's. Her fascination with paint and its uses is matched by several of her fellow quilt artists. As already mentioned, Pamela Studstill patterns her cloth with paint and Risë Nagin uses paint in her work. Therese May boldly paints directly onto her cloth, creating thick, often crusty, surfaces of layered color and texture. May regards the time spent sewing a quilt, which can easily add up to

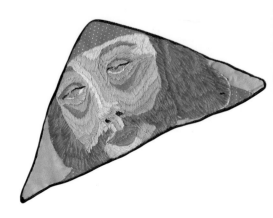

Detail from plate 6.

65

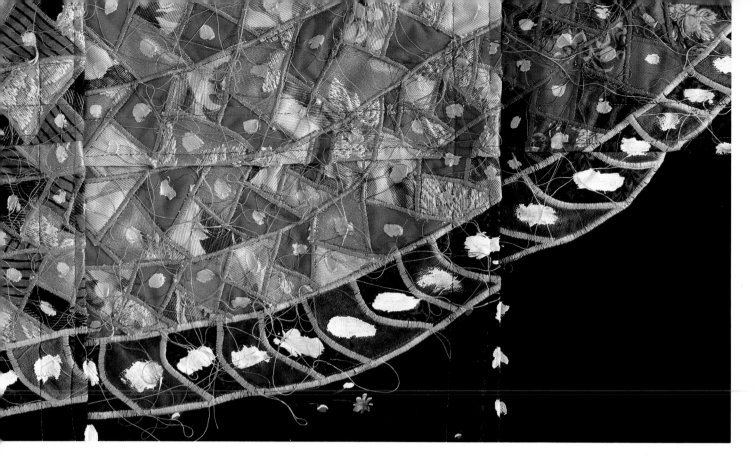

Detail from plate 20.

Detail from plate 19.

dozens of hours, as therapeutic, but she also enjoys the risk of adding paint to it. "Adding paint can either make or break the work. You can lose a lot of time if the paint you add doesn't work.."

Several of the quilt artists regularly dye their own fabrics. The leading exponent of this approach is Jan Myers-Newbury, who uses nothing but her own procion-dyed cloth (left). As contemporary quiltmakers have struggled to find gradations of color required by their works, many are studying dyeing processes so that they, too, can create with a theoretically unlimited palate. Pauline Burbidge and Joan Schulze are also experienced at fabric dyeing and they have used it extensively in their work. Artists Gayle Fraas and Duncan Slade are well-known for painting with dyes, creating rich yet luminescent surfaces. Also painting with dye in highly individualistic ways is Yvonne Porcella, whose workshops, like those of Fraas and Slade, are always filled with students wanting to learn her techniques. In addition to painting and dyeing, Jean Hewes often makes batiks and Risë Nagin stains some of her fabrics. The approach of quilt artist Ruth McDowell is quite different, however: "Using patterned, commercially available fabric ties my quilts to human life. Making art out of the sort of fabrics that people wear and use every day pleases me. I don't have any interest in dyeing, or painting on fabric, which would remove my work a step away from people."

Other techniques regularly employed by members of the group are color photocopying, as practiced by Joan Schulze and Terrie

Hancock Mangat, cyanotyping, again used by Joan Schulze, and fabric stamping (or stenciling) as practiced by Deborah Felix.[116]

Up until very recently, the "finished look" was an integral feature of any "fine" quilt. This "look" dictated that all fabric raw edges were covered, all loose threads were clipped and all seams were sewn neatly. As many of the artists have expanded the subject matter depicted in quilts, they have, in order to accomplish this feat, added techniques, violating all the tenets of the "finished look." Therese May's works are a maze of loose threads, often held to their surfaces by bold applications of paint (facing page, top). "I'm basically a rebel," admits May. "I've done pristine work and I'm good at it. It's not that I can't be neat. I simply enjoy expressing myself differently from the crowd." She and Jean Hewes often leave fabric raw edges exposed (right), lending their works added dimensionality. "Unfinished edges give a forceful, primitive look I like," says Hewes. "It's not slick or smooth." Several of the artists have reversed fabric, using the back as the primary surface.

As in many media, quilt artists are also layering their materials. Painters have done this for centuries, building up thin layers to produce, among other characteristics, luminescence. Quilt artists Veronica Fitzgerald, Jean Hewes and Risë Hagin have layered thin over broad, and transparent over dense, fabrics to create illusive

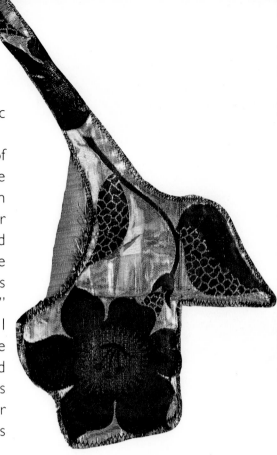

Detail from plate 2.

Detail from plate 15.

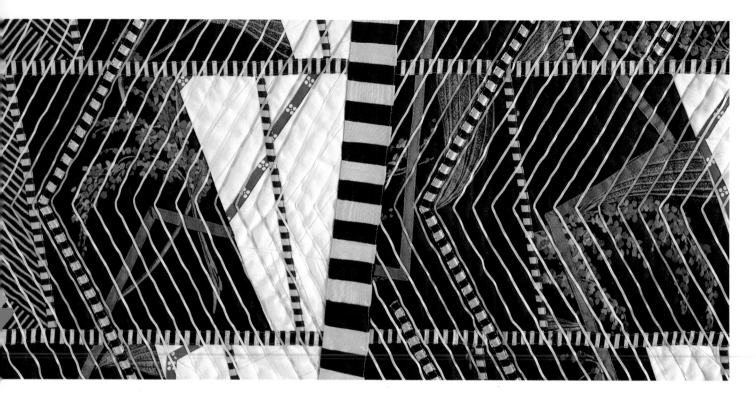

Detail from plate 23.

qualities on the surfaces of their quilts (this page and page 64). Jan Myers-Newbury has created the same visual effect in her work (page 66) by piecing a lattice weave into the surface of her quilt.

As quilt artists have experimented with techniques and materials, it is only logical that they have questioned the standard format of a quilt. Yvonne Porcella's giant, three-dimensional kimono (plate 7), Gayle Fraas and Duncan Slade's three-dimensional folding screens (plates 4 and 13), Joan Schulze's free-hanging, double-sided quilts (plates 11 and 17) and Ruth McDowell's two-dimensional quilt with its three-dimensional projections (plate 10) challenge the traditional precept that quilts are, by definition, flat, one-sided two-dimensional objects. Porcella is quite matter-of-fact in her views: "The more quilt artists show their work, the more that work will challenge the traditional definition of the quilt. And the more we will grow. As we grow, the art world will be forced to react. Therefore, getting beyond bed-size is good. It is forcing us to innovate."

"Getting beyond bed-size" is certainly what these quilt artists have done. It is vitally important that readers note the sizes of these quilts. They are among the largest ever created: all match, and often exceed, the size of other large modern artworks. It is one thing, as any artist knows, to be creative within traditionally accepted limits; it is quite another to maintain quality while expanding scale. "What's happening here couldn't have occurred in a small, traditional format," says Joan Schulze. With these works, the quilt has expanded beyond the confines of functional object in a forceful, unmistakable way.

AS QUILT ARTISTS continue to challenge the quilt medium, experimenting with its various facets, they risk alienating their current audience—the quilt world—before they have gained the admiration of the art establishment. Thus, as outcasts from one world, unaccepted by another, they may find themselves residing in a state of artistic limbo.

Ideally, these quilt artists will remain an integral part of the quilt world as they receive recognition in the art world, to the benefit of all quiltmakers. Without these artists, quiltmaking could find itself lacking enough bothersome, progressive pioneers to disturb yet nourish the traditional terrain. The art world could survive their absence, but it would be the poorer without them. The quilt world, on the other hand, could suffer a demise similar to that undergone after World War II if it decides it has had enough of these "cultural renegades."

The quilt artists are mixed in their forecasts of what is to come. Some, like Fitzgerald and James, are worried, sensing that they are standing at a literal crossroads in their careers. Their deepest fear is most forcefully enunciated in Deborah Felix's comment that "there's a stereotype about quilts. They're seen as 'just something women do.' Quilts are not going to be accepted as an art form for a long time." Others share the almost defiant attitude displayed in statements by Jan Myers-Newbury and Nancy Crow. Says Myers-Newbury, "I've found the thing I was meant to do in my life. I'm not going to quit." Crow adds, "I'm going to continue making quilts because I'm driven. I fully believe that the quilt's time has come; only the fact that it's made from fabric has held it back until now." With the recent breakdown of barriers between certain parts of the art and art/craft worlds and the borrowing among media that has resulted, Bernice Steinbaum, a New York City art dealer who represents Miriam Schapiro, among others, boldly predicts that quilts will be the next medium to break through and achieve status in the art world. Says Steinbaum, "In the not-too-distant future, art quilts will grace the walls of leading galleries around the world." Steinbaum's prediction is a welcome one to a group of artists who know their time has come, but wait, wondering if anyone else has noticed.

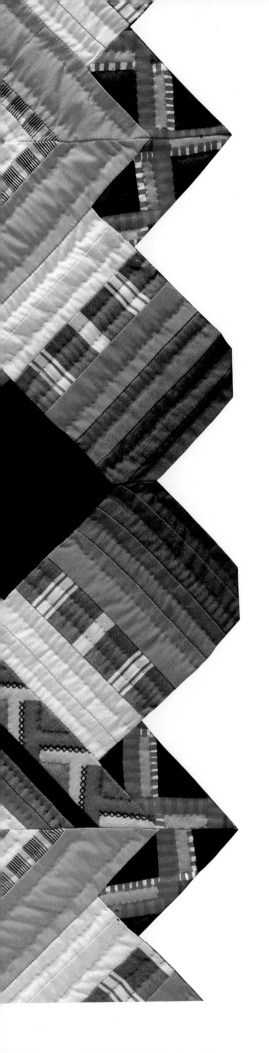

THE QUILTS

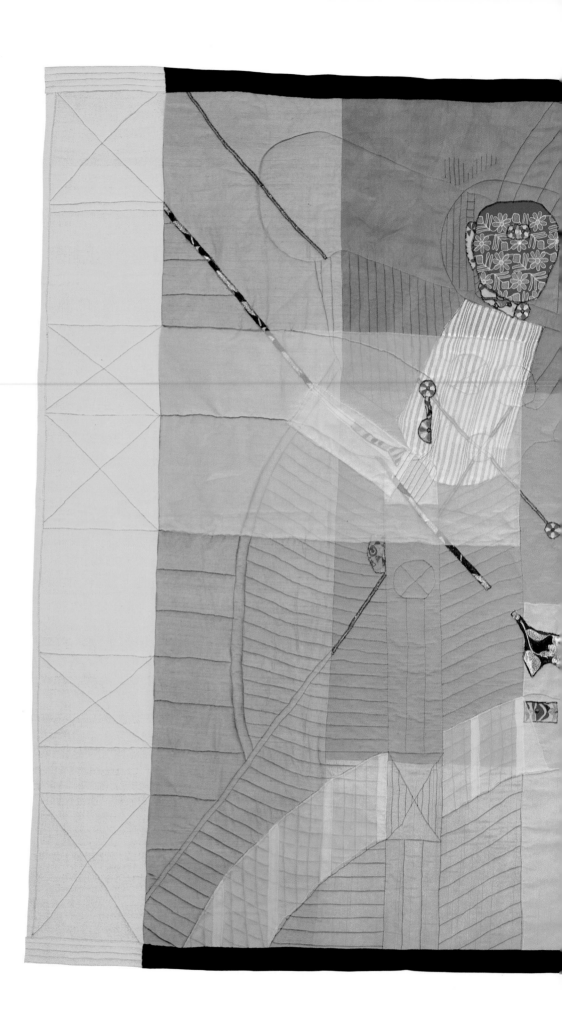

Plate 2.
JEAN HEWES
Shooting Star, 87 × 121 inches

Plate 3.
THERESE MAY
Thy Will Be Done, 88 × 91 ½ inches

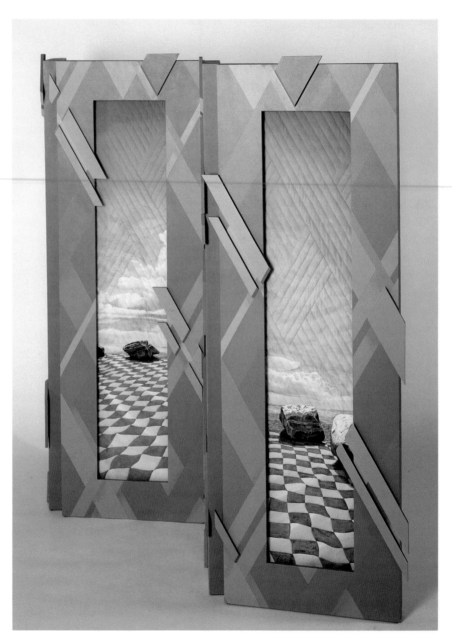

Side view

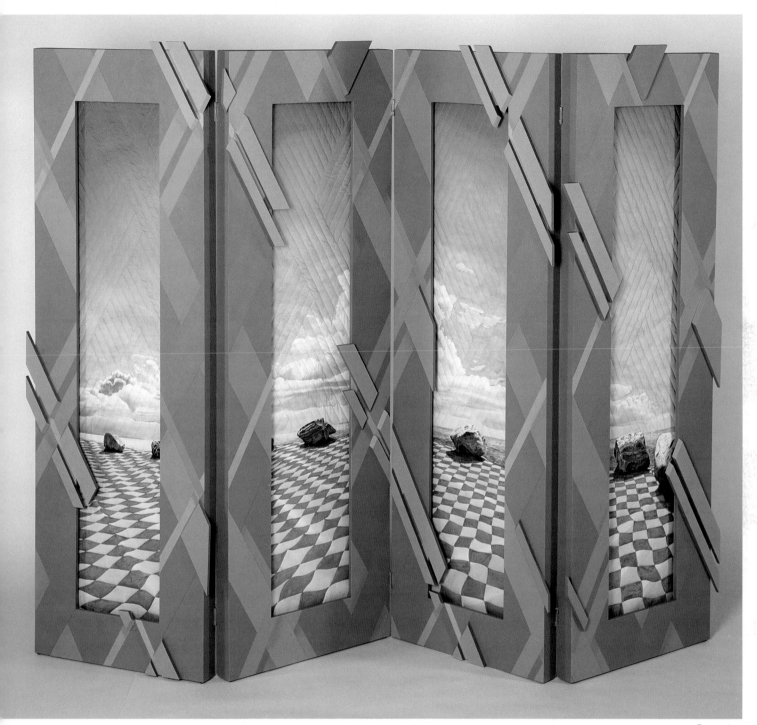

Front view

Plate 4.
GAYLE FRAAS AND DUNCAN SLADE
The Precipice, four panels, each measuring 72 × 24 × 3 inches excluding projections
Collection of Ardis and Robert James

Plate 5.
PAMELA STUDSTILL
#49, 60½ × 84½ inches

Plate 6.
TERRIE HANCOCK MANGAT
*Dashboard Saints: in memory of Saint
Christopher (Who lost his magnetism. . .),
99 × 123 inches
Collection of Ardis and Robert James*

Back view

Plate 7.
YVONNE PORCELLA
Snow on Mount Fuji, 132 × 86 × 14 inches
Collection of the American Craft Museum, New York, New York

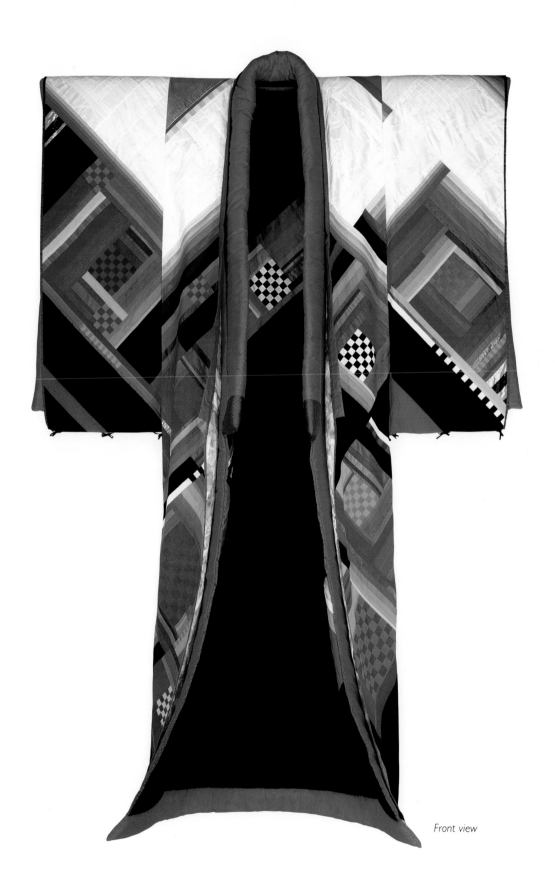

Front view

Plate 8.
JEAN HEWES
Angel, 87½ × 82 inches

Plate 9.
PAULINE BURBIDGE
Spirals I, 88 × 88 inches
Collection of Ardis and Robert James

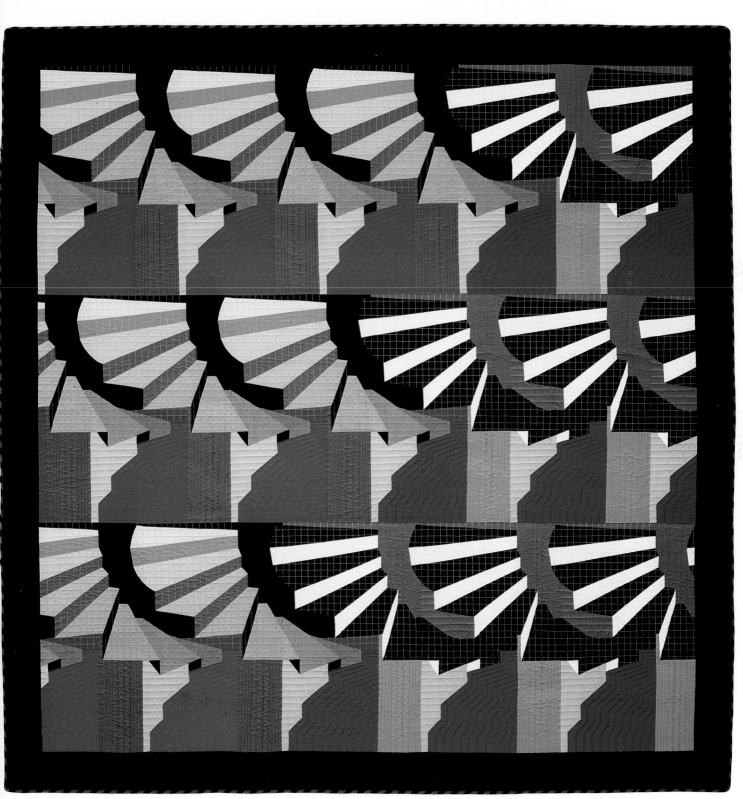

Plate 10.
RUTH B. McDOWELL
Waterlilies—Nymphaea odorata, 95 × 156 inches

Angle view

Front view

Plate 11.
JOAN SCHULZE
The Marriage: Woman/Man, 96 × 111 × 36 inches

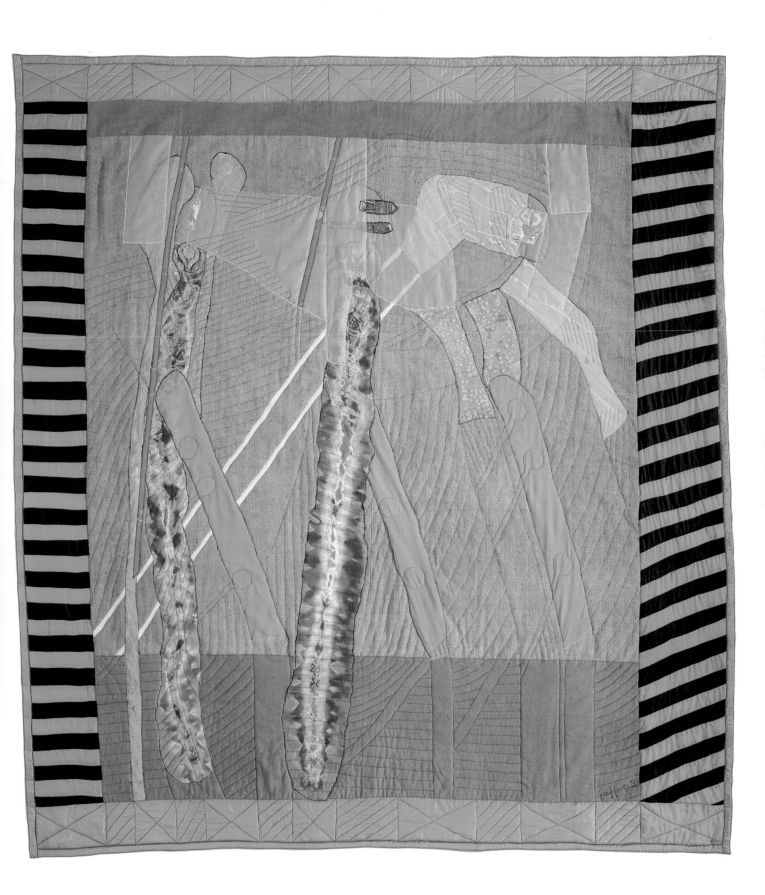

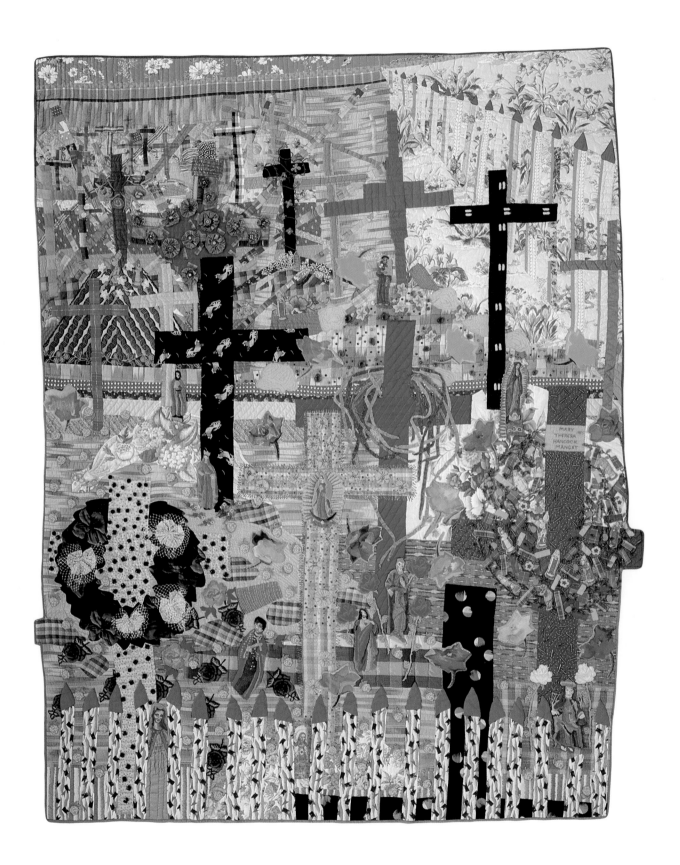

Plate 16.
PAULINE BURBIDGE
Spirals II, 87 1/2 × 84 inches
Collection of Ardis and Robert James

Back view

Plate 17.
JOAN SCHULZE
Self-Portrait, 92 × 73 inches

Front view

Plate 18.
RISË NAGIN
On the Road with Marsden and Sonia, 75 1/4 × 97 1/2 inches

Plate 19.
JAN MYERS-NEWBURY
Depth of Field III: Plane View,
84 × 131 ½ inches
Collection of Ardis and
Robert James

Plate 20.
THERESE MAY
For All the World to See, 85 × 89 inches
Collection of John Walsh III

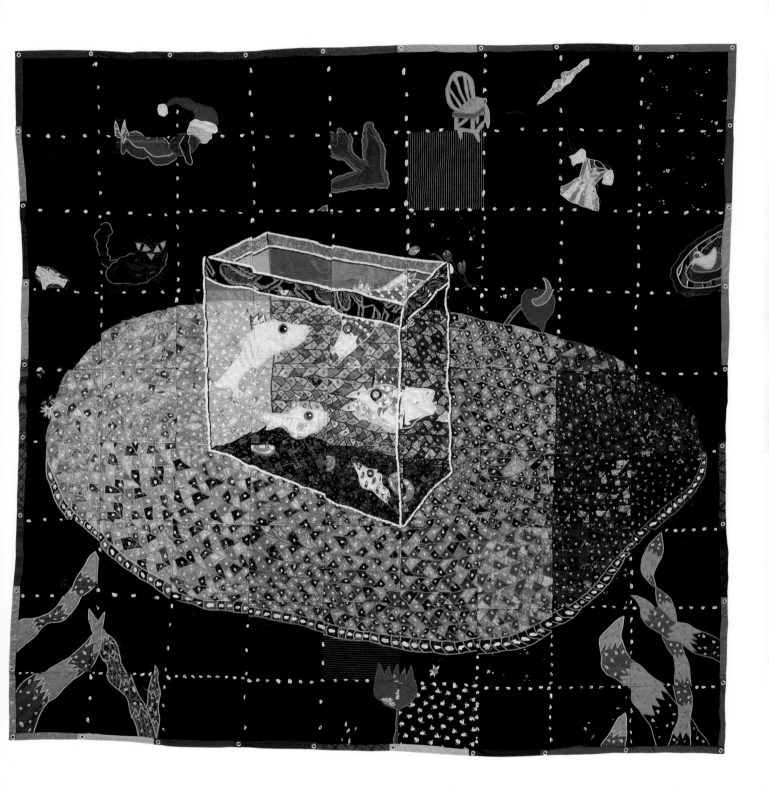

Plate 21.
PAMELA STUDSTILL
#47, 60 1/2 × 84 1/2 inches
Collection of Ardis and Robert James

Plate 22.
DEBORAH J. FELIX
Discussing Plants for the Future, 69 × 90 inches

Plate 24.
NANCY CROW
Lady of Guadalupe, 81 1/2 × 59 inches

THUNDER CREEK
ROAD
WILLOW RIVER
Willow Rapids
BR 1561
1559
1594
BM 1615
WILLOW
ROAD
BM 1621
1556
Little Rice River
LYNNE
1592

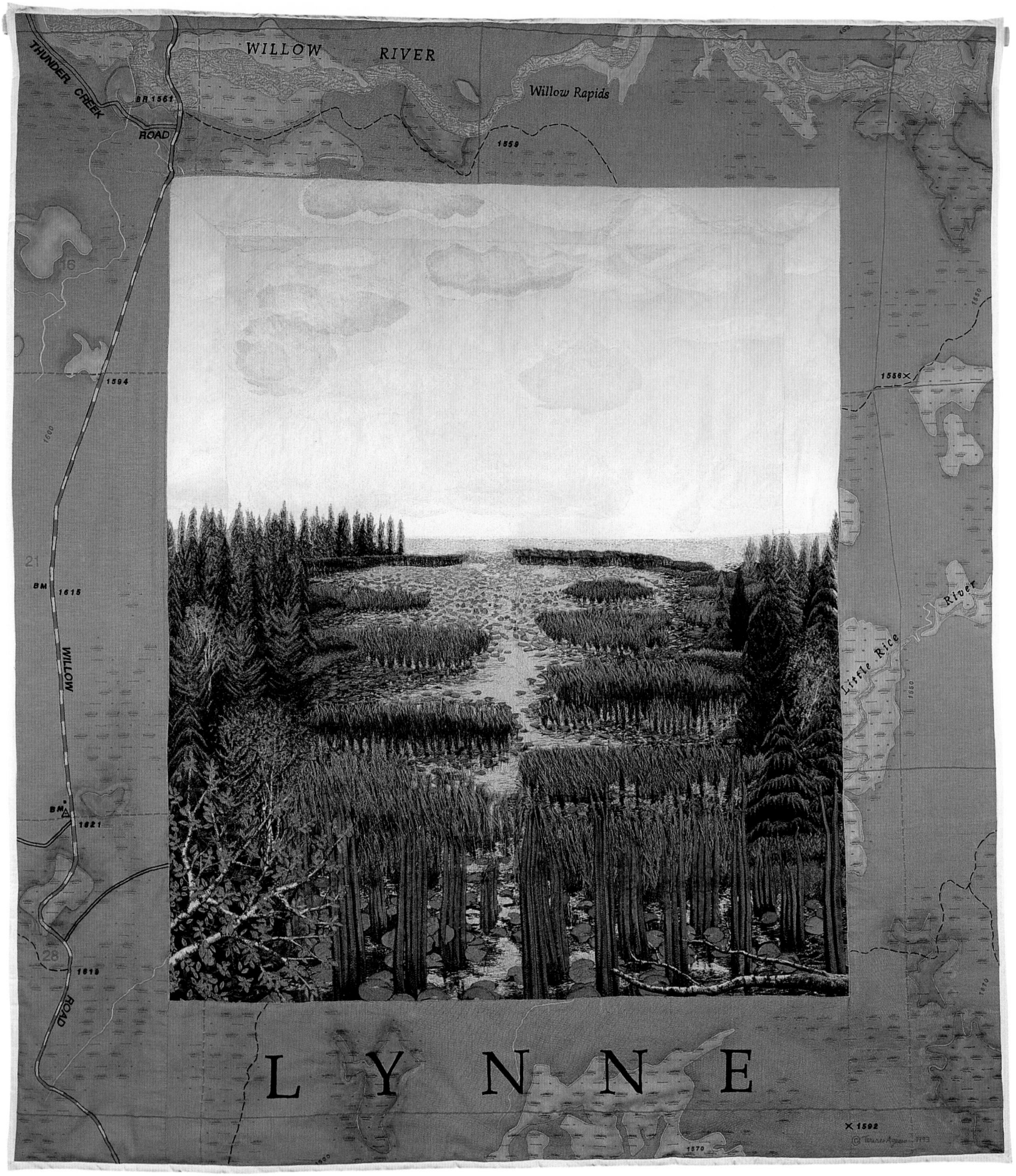

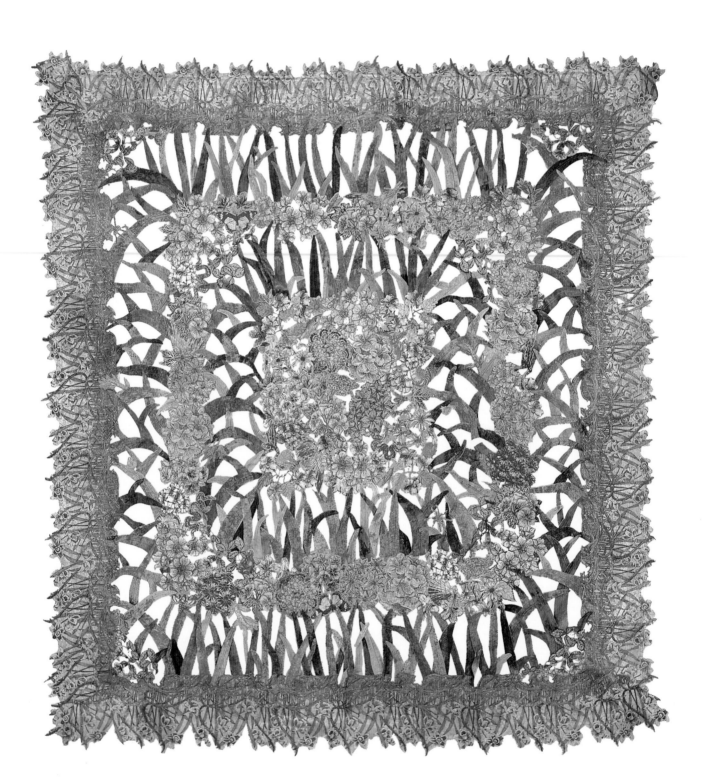

Plate 27.
M. JOAN LINTAULT
In the Grass, 91 × 98 inches
Collection of John M. Walsh

Plate 28.
PAULINE BURBIDGE
Nottingham Reflections, 80 × 80 inches
Collection of John M. Walsh

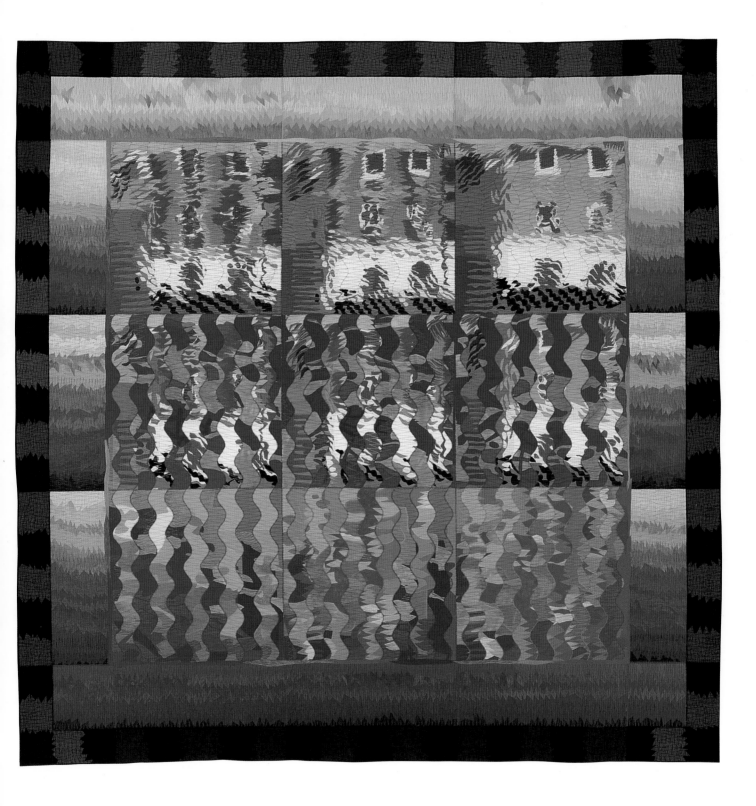

FOOTNOTES

1. Emery, "The Vital Things," p. 13. For additional interior photographs of a late-Victorian home, see also McMorris, "Victorian Style," pp. 26–33.

2. Mrs. M.E.W. Sherwood, quoted in Lynes, *The Tastemakers*, p. 105.

3. Leiser, "Simplicity," p. 229.

4. Leiser, p. 225.

5. Elsie de Wolfe, *The House in Good Taste* (New York: Century & Co., 1913), quoted in Anscombe, *A Woman's Touch*, p. 72.

6. Emery, p. 13.

7. As early as 1855, *Godey's Lady's Magazine* (October 1855, p. 381) announced to its readers, "Patchwork quilts, unless in silks, are rarely seen in cities, the glory of our grandmothers having passed away." And by 1882 *Harper's Bazar* ("Patchwork," September 16, 1882, p. 583) declared that "silk has superseded all material less rich and costly." See McMorris, *Crazy Quilts*, p. 11.

8. *Arthur's Home Magazine*, July 1884, p. 424.

9. Lanigan, "Revival," p. 19.

10. Bruce, "Appliqué Patchwork," p. 13.

11. *Patchwork and Quilt Making*, n.p.

12. Arts and Crafts reformers sought to revive the delicate embroidery style of the Middle Ages which had been replaced by a coarser, more needlepoint-like wool embroidery called Berlin Work, popular from 1830 to 1870. They founded the Royal School of Art Needlework in London in 1872 to raise the artistic status of embroidery and provide an income-producing skill for needy gentlewomen. By the 1880's, the Art Needlework movement had spread to the United States. We see its effect in the great amount of embroidery used on late-Victorian silk quilts.

13. Blair, "Collectors' Interests," p. 164.

14. Bruce, p. 13.

15. Bruce, p. 13. Wealthy patrons commissioned embroidered panels, curtains and bedspreads for their homes, and embroidery was exhibited as art in Arts and Crafts exhibitions and international fairs such as the 1876 Centennial Exhibition in Philadelphia.

16. Webster, *Quilts*, p. xvii.

17. The resulting project was of mixed success, but a well-known magazine's sponsorship of original quilt designs by artists demonstrates that the traditional "rules" of quiltmaking were yet to be firmly re-established. The first quilt in the series, a wild-animal quilt by Ernest Thompson Seton, identified only as the author of *Wild Animals I Have Known*, is typical of the difficulty of the quilts in the series, each designed by an artist with little or no understanding of the difficulties involved in translating a drawing into appliqué. For his part, Seton rather smugly assured readers that his quilt would "be a delight to the workers who had patience to finish it." The complexity of Seton's quilt—child's play compared to the May issue's "Dragon Bedquilt" that some 1905 subscribers may be working on still—seemed to have undone even the magazine editors. In a special note, they admitted as much: "It is impossible for us to supply any patterns for this quilt," they wrote. "When the design was originally made by Mr. Seton for *The Journal* it was our intention to offer to supply patterns. But the practical obstacles [ed. translation—it was too difficult] presented themselves, making it impossible to do this. All that can be told, then, about the quilt is told here." (*Ladies' Home Journal*, January 1905, p. 9.)

18. *Needlecraft Magazine*, July 1927, quoted in "Gleanings from Aunt Laura's Scrapbook," *Quilter's Newsletter Magazine*, January 1984, p. 37.

19. Lewis F. Day, *Art in Needlework* (1900), quoted in Bath, *Needlework in America*, p. 38.

20. The unwavering popularity of the Colonial style can be seen in virtually all modern-day decorating magazines: advertisements for Colonial reproduction furniture, house plans for Colonial salt-box homes and articles on Colonial decorating tips abound. Several modern-day magazines are devoted solely to the Colonial style, more than a half-century after the beginning of the Colonial revival.

21. One early collector wrote of intentionally returning home from collecting excursions under the cover of darkness, so her neighbors would not notice her staggering in with old maple tables and think her strange. She recalled searching through an old lady's barn and discovering a highboy in perfect condition but for two missing drawers. "We looked for them high and low," she said, "until finally we discovered that the old lady had used them for window boxes and had planted pansies in them." But she bought them all. (Lockwood, *Decoration*, p. 159.)

22. Lynes, p. 240.

23. *Good Housekeeping*, April 1928, as quoted in Lasansky, *In the Heart of Pennsylvania*, p. 95.

24. Lynes, pp. 238–239.

25. Finley, *Old Patchwork Quilts*, p. 22.

26. *Patchwork and Quilt Making*, n.p. There were, besides the already-mentioned Webster and Finley texts, Carlie Sexton's books: *Early American Quilts* (1924), *Old Fashioned Quilts* (1928) and *Yesterday's Quilts in Homes of Today* (1930); Carrie A. Hall and Rose G. Kretsinger's *The Romance of the Patchwork Quilt in America* (1935) with its useful display of quilt blocks from Hall's collection; Alice Beyer's *Quilting* (1934); as well as how-to brochures published by manufacturers of quilting supplies.

27. Lockwood, p. 148.

28. *Patchwork and Quilt Making*, n.p.

29. Parker and Pollock, *Old Mistresses*, p. 65.

30. [Advertisement], *Ladies' Home Journal*, II (March 1885), 6.

31. [Advertisement for Ladies Art Co.], *Ladies' Home Journal,* XXII (December 1904), 52.

32. Allen, *The Big Change,* p. 119.

33. *Patchwork Quilts: How to Make Them,* n.p.

34. *Grandma Dexter,* Book no. 36B, p. 2.

35. *Grandmother Clark's Oldfashioned,* p. 2.

36. The *Prairie Farmer* newspaper of Chicago printed a pattern called *King Tut's Crown* in 1931 (Brackman, *Encyclopedia,* III, 172) and the *Chicago Tribune* ran *Cleopatra's Puzzle* in their syndicated Nancy Cabot quilt column (Brackman, *Encyclopedia,* III, 172). Both newspaper patterns were variations of *Robbing Peter to Pay Paul.*

37. There were patterns called *Indian Squares, Indian Maze, Indian Mats, Arrowheads, Navajo* and a fan design called *Mohawk Trail.* The *Kansas City Star* gave readers *Indian Trail* in 1931 (Brackman, *Encyclopedia,* III, 160) and *Indian Canoes* in 1933 (Brackman, *Encyclopedia,* III, 150). And Grandmother Clark, not to be outdone, used a *Double Wedding Ring* variation called *Indian Wedding Ring* on the cover of her 1932 catalogue.

38. *Progressive Farmer* ran a *Lindbergh's Night Flight* quilt pattern (Brackman, *Encyclopedia,* II, 92), while the Nancy Cabot quilt column gave readers patterns for *Spirit of St. Louis* (Brackman, *Encyclopedia,* III, 136) and *Lindy's Plane* (Brackman, *Encyclopedia,* V, 318). In addition to these Lindbergh-inspired designs, there were a great number of patterns with chunky, stylized airplanes or central designs resembling propellers. Many of these were printed in *The Kansas City Star,* including *The Airplane* (Brackman, *Encyclopedia,* II, 92) and *Air-Ship Propeller* (Brackman, *Encyclopedia,* VII, 474), which are illustrated on page 34 of this book.

39. "Patches for Robes," *The Household Magazine,* February 1931, as reprinted in *Quilter's Newsletter Magazine,* July/August 1984, p. 46.

40. Brackman, "Record Breaking Quilts," p. 5.

41. Allen Harding, "Why We Have Gone Mad Over Crossword Puzzles," *The American Magazine,* March 1925, p. 28, quoted in Mowry, *The Twenties,* p. 73.

42. Hall and Kretsinger, p. 80.

43. Brackman, *Encyclopedia,* I, 32.

44. Shannon, *Between the Wars,* p. 138.

45. Bush, *The Streamlined Decade,* p. 167.

46. In the New York City Museum of Modern Art's 1934 exhibition "Machine Art," such useful yet beautiful objects as cameras, barometers, alarm clocks, ball bearings, springs and gears were displayed for exemplary design. Much earlier, in what seems even now a startling exhibition, the Newark (N.J.) Museum set out to prove that beauty was not related to price, rarity or age by displaying a room full of bathtubs (1915).

47. *Designs Worth Doing,* Fall/Winter 1931–32, p. 26.

48. McKim's flower series stands out because the flowers were meant to be sewn by machine rather than, as are most floral designs, to be appliquéd by hand. McKim's catalogue entry for one of the designs emphasizes this fact: "The pieced poppy is all straight sewing, the sort that may be run up on the sewing machine. . . . Really quite simple to make." (*Designs Worth Doing,* Fall/Winter 1931–32, p. 18.) It is her necessarily straight edges and her use of an oblong block instead of the more traditional square block that give her flower designs a decidedly machine-age look. It is interesting that McKim was to have an impact upon quiltmakers in the 1970's who recognized the quality of her quilt designs and were attracted to her *One Hundred and One Patchwork Patterns.*

49. Lynes, p. 249.

50. Advertisement for Model Brassière Co., *Vogue,* p. 106.

51. Jenkins, *The Thirties,* p. 34.

52. Allen, *Since Yesterday,* p. 112.

53. Ruby McKim wrote, "If quilts have taken the country by storm, then the hexagon Flower Garden . . .—well, it's a whirlwind!" (*Designs Worth Doing,* Fall/Winter 1931–32, p. 20.)

54. McCrea, "Good Ideas," p. 8.

55. *Grandma Dexter,* Book no. 36B, p. 2.

56. Manufacturers promoted the idea that, even in modern times, women could find time to produce a family heirloom with the help of a quilt kit. Read an advertisement in *House Beautiful,* "If . . . you'd like to hand down to posterity a patchwork quilt, you can very easily do so by purchasing the patches ready cut, and sewing them together on a machine." (LXV, January 1929, p. 9.) Many of the most popular quilt designs of the 1930's were available in ready-cut form, often advertised with exaggerated claims for the speed with which they could be assembled. The Needlecraft Supply Co., for example, said that sewing together the 2,474 squares in its *Double Irish Chain* kit would require "but a few hours of pleasant work." (*Patchwork Quilts,* n.p.) By 1928, the Ladies Art Co. offered over five hundred designs that could be mail-ordered pre-sewn. Prices ranged from thirty-five cents to two dollars for one quilt block. Whole tops cost twenty-five to forty-five dollars. In the 1930's, appliqué kits became popular and women could buy ready-cut kits of the prize-winning appliqués from the 1933 World's Fair quilt contest sponsored by Sears, Roebuck.

57. Hall and Kretsinger, p. 17.

58. Hall and Kretsinger, p. 28.

59. Beam, "Streamlining," p. 74.

60. "Wherever We Look," p. 4.

61. Moyers, "Listening to America," p. 109.

62. Hooper, "The Real Change," p. 105.

63. "Mail Order Catalogue," p. 67. Less than twenty years later, Brand's focus would change from living without technology to living with it, as he edited the *Whole Earth Software Catalog.*

64. Leiser, p. 227.

65. "The Quest for Spiritual Survival," p. 24.

66. Ruskin as quoted in Naylor, *The Arts and Crafts Movement,* p. 28. An award in John Ruskin's name is given every year by the English Crafts Council to honor leading craftspeople. Quilt artist Pauline Burbidge received the award in 1982.

67. Brown, *Creative Quilting,* p. 133.

68. Reyner Banham, *Theory and Design in the First Machine Age* (The Architectural Press, 1960), p. 12, quoted in Naylor, p. 10.

69. Fisher, *Living for Today,* p. 11.

70. James S. Plaut, foreword to Octavio Paz, *In Praise of Hands,* p. 11.

71. The quilt co-operatives that were organized in the late 1960's were often sponsored by VISTA workers. Although they were begun simultaneously in many parts of the country, the longest-lived were in Appalachia, the South and the Dakotas. Some of these co-ops, in addition to Mountain Artisans and Cabin Creek Quilts, were the Blue Ridge Hearthside Crafts Association of Sugar Grove, North Carolina, the Freedom Quilting Bee of Alberta, Alabama, and Dakotah Handcrafts of Sisseton, South Dakota. The co-ops provided an income to women who pieced quilts, drapery yardages, tablecloths and pillow tops which were then sold in fashionable department stores. Cabin Creek Quilts, for example, was started by coal miners' widows who had been living on as little as three hundred dollars a year.

72. Laury, *Applique Stitchery*, p. 16.

73. Laury, *Applique Stitchery*, p. 11.

74. Brown, p. 18.

75. Brown, p. 10.

76. For more information about the Freedom Quilting Bee, see Callahan, " 'Helping the Peoples,' " pp. 20–29.

77. *House Beautiful*, May 1970, p. 139.

78. "Nostalgia," *Newsweek*, p. 38.

79. "Nostalgia," *Life*, p. 39.

80. "Nostalgia," *Newsweek*, p. 34. Oz mania was already so strong in 1970 that a fan paid $15,000 for the ruby slippers Judy Garland had worn in the MGM *Wizard of Oz* production.

81. Also revived were such superheroes of the past as Popeye, Superman, Tarzan, Batman, Sherlock Holmes and Wonder Woman. Not everyone was enthusiastic about the revivalist spirit of the 1970's. Poet Archibald MacLeish, for example, confessed to being puzzled by the whole nostalgia boom. "I am mystified about this current nostalgia for the '20s," he said. "I remember that period well, and I found it pretty boring." ("Why the Craze," p. 76.) One satirist even proposed that the country was on the verge of running out of old times to bring back. "It isn't that the days are going by too quickly; they're coming back too fast," he warned. "The Twenties, a veritable mother lode of memories, are very nearly depleted. The Thirties, never a rich decade, are also overworked. As for the Forties, few people long for a war right now, and that puts us well into the Fifties, a scant fifteen years ago.... We are now dealing with shoddy, inferior nostalgia and it simply won't stand the use.... Because it wears out so fast we'll soon be saying, 'You think that was something? You should have been alive ten minutes ago!' " (Heath, "Nostalgia Shock," p. 18.)

82. Tyrmand, "Reflections," p. 56.

83. *Quilter's Newsletter Magazine*, September 1971, p. 3.

84. Kramer, "Art," p. 22.

85. Malcolm, "On and Off," 1971, p. 60.

86. Shapiro, "American Quilts," pp. 43–44.

87. Other museum quilt exhibitions in 1971 were the Baltimore Museum of Art's "The Great American Cover-Up: Counterpanes of the 18th and 19th Centuries," which included coverlets as well as quilts, and was organized by Dena Katzenberg; an exhibition of over 150 antique quilts mounted by the Chester County Historical Society in West Chester, Pennsylvania; and an exhibition held at Berea College in Kentucky called "Patchwork Quilts of the Southern Highlands," which *House Beautiful* (November 1971, p. 82) recommended to "everyone into the rage for patchwork."

88. "A Stitch in Another Time," p. 60.

89. "Op: Adventure Without Danger," p. 83.

90. Laury, *Quilts & Coverlets*, p. 11.

91. Mayor Lindsay declared March 24 to April 1, 1973, Craft Week in New York City. And one retailer explained why craft items were being given more shelf space in her store: "Fashion has gotten too faddy. One day the midi; one day hot pants. Needlework is a nice, safe thing." (Bender, "Craft Comeback," p. 2.)

92. "Hobbies Boom," p. 33.

93. Bender, p. 2.

94. Leonore Fleischer, editor at Ballantine Books, quoted in Bender, p. 2.

95. "Craft Comeback," *House & Garden*, p. 115.

96. Corbin, "Notes to Help You," p. 12.

97. "The Booming Business," p. 66.

98. Interview with Cecelia Toth of *Good Housekeeping*, August 19, 1985.

99. An earlier exhibition, combining contemporary quilts and wood crafts, was the De Cordova (Lincoln, Mass.) Museum's "Bed and Board," held from June 21 to September 28, 1975. Quilt artist Michael James had two quilts in this exhibition. From April 10 to May 20, 1976, the Pratt Graphics Center Gallery in New York City displayed "Printed Quilts, Quilted Prints," a show of contemporary quilts featuring hand-printed designs. Both of these exhibitions were accompanied by catalogues, as was "The New American Quilt," an exhibition on display from April 1 to June 13, 1976.

100. Another exhibition linking "fine" artists and quiltmakers was the traveling show "Artist's [sic] Quilts," which opened at the La Jolla (Calif.) Museum of Contemporary Art on January 23, 1981. Eighteen quilts were made by needlewomen following the designs and fabric selections of ten artists.

101. Christo's monumental works are probably the largest ever made using fabric. In order to sew his *Valley Curtain*, which stretched briefly between two mountain slopes in Colorado, sewers spread the fabric out across a factory floor and moved their sewing machines from position to position. The finished "curtain" was so large it took two weeks merely to fold it.

102. Emont-Scott, *Alan Shields*, p. 18.

103. Robins, "Anne Healy," p. 129.

104. The *Log Cabin* quilt used in *Bed* once belonged to artist Dorothea Rockburne. She recalls, "It was kind of special to me because I had it at the time my daughter Christine was born, and she used to spend a lot of time on it. I didn't actually give Bob the quilt, it just sort of appeared in the work one day. We were living at Black Mountain College then, and when you sent the wash out things had a way of appearing and disappearing. I remember when I first saw the painting he had made of it I thought, 'Oh! That's the quilt that I had.' It was a wonderful experience seeing it. Years later the painting had to be restored and I remember seeing it in an exhibition, and they had made the pillows too puffy, and had to take some of

the stuffing out." (Interview, September 6, 1985.)

105. Beneš had the *Fan* quilt hanging in his studio for a while and admired the feeling of movement in it. "It's such an incredible thing," says Beneš about the quilt. "I wanted to get that movement going in my work. I didn't copy it exactly, [because] I couldn't do as good a job as that old lady." (Interview, September 9, 1985.)

106. Miriam Schapiro has long championed the idea that women's needlework was and is an art form. She has said, "Through the whole domestic range of things that are produced—the tea cozies, the doilies, the mats, the antimacassars, clothing and quilts—in all of that there's got to be the impulse toward making something beautiful. And that impulse is the impulse of the artist." (Interview, November 4, 1985.) She regularly incorporates bits of needlework which she has found or been given. *Wonderland* is full of needlework mementoes gathered on a trip to Australia.

107. Doherty, *Dynamic Still Lifes*, p. 12. Art historian Linda Nochlin has written, "The patchwork quilt has recently become a burning issue in certain feminist art circles." ("Feminism and Formal Innovation in the Work of Miriam Schapiro," in Gouma-Peterson, *Miriam Schapiro*, p. 22.) Many women artists in the mid-seventies experimented with grid designs and symbols taken from quilts. Patsy Norvell made one "quilt" of locks of hair saved from giving friends haircuts, another from the vinyl ruffles used to decorate shelf edges. Margaret Wharton made a "crazy quilt" out of crushed soft-drink cans in 1973. (See her *Heirloom* on page 58.)

108. Letter from David Schirm to Penny McMorris, September 1985.

109. Kaufman's quilt was shown at the Bernice Steinbaum Gallery from May 1 to June 1, 1985, in a one-woman show entitled "The Decorative Aesthetic: Embroidered & Beaded Crazy Quilt & Screens." Another early gallery exhibition in New York City that included quilts was the Monique Knowlton Gallery's "Edward Larson: Windtoys, Woodcarvings & Picture Quilts," which showed this contemporary folk artist's work from December 9, 1980 to January 7, 1981.

110. Quilts were now shown on walls as aesthetic objects, rather than for their historical interest or technical achievements, in the same way paintings are displayed. We are not implying that quilts were not displayed vertically before: they were, in fair exhibitions and in museums.

111. The typical crazy quilt, unlike its cotton counterpart, was made more for beauty than for use. It was made of fragile materials and embellished with embroidery, paint and beads, and so was not washable. It was made without batting, tied rather than quilted, not made to keep sleepers warm.

112. Both the traditional *Log Cabin* and crazy quilt blocks are constructed of fabric pieces which are sewn onto foundation cloths. (See Fox, "The Log Cabin," pp. 6–13.)

113. The Missouri Historical Society's collection contains a quilt embellished with taxidermically stuffed birds and chipmunks. For a photograph see McMorris, *Crazy Quilts*, p. 51.

114. Although there were trained, professional designers of quilt patterns, such as Ruby McKim, most innovations in quilt design came from needlewomen who had no professional training.

115. Most major New York City modern art galleries now show the work of at least one artist working in ceramics. However, many ceramists would insist that their work has not been accepted by the art establishment, linking their plight to that of all fiber artists.

116. Felix served an apprenticeship at Philadelphia's The Fabric Workshop, a non-profit visual arts organization founded in 1977 to promote experimental and innovative fabric design and printing and to educate the public about textiles as an art form. Pattern painters Cynthia Carlson, Joyce Kozloff, Robert Kushner, Kim MacConnel and Miriam Schapiro were all artists in residence there during the late 1970's.

BIBLIOGRAPHY

Allen, Frederick Lewis. *The Big Change: America Transforms Itself 1900–1950.* New York: Harper & Row, Publishers, 1952.

Allen, Frederick Lewis. *Since Yesterday: The 1930s in America.* New York: Harper & Row, Publishers, 1939.

Anscombe, Isabelle. *A Woman's Touch: Women in Design from 1860 to the Present Day.* New York: Elisabeth Sifton Books, The Viking Press, 1984.

Arthur's Home Magazine, July 1884, p. 424.

Banham, Reyner. *Design by Choice.* New York: Rizzoli, 1981.

Bath, Virginia Churchill. *Needlework in America: History, Designs and Techniques.* New York: The Viking Press, 1979.

Beam, Ethel. "Streamlining the Art of Quilting," *House Beautiful,* XCVIII (August 1956), 74–77.

Benberry, Cuesta. "The 20th Century's First Quilt Revival," *Quilter's Newsletter Magazine,* X (July/August 1979), 20–21+; X (September 1979), 25–26+; X (October 1979), 10–11+.

Bender, Marylin. "Craft Comeback," *The New York Times,* March 28, 1971, Sec. 3, p. 2.

Beyer, Alice. *Quilting.* Chicago: South Park Commissioners, Recreation Department, 1934.

Bishop, Robert, and Patricia Coblentz. *American Decorative Arts: 360 Years of Creative Design.* New York: Harry N. Abrams, Inc., Publishers, 1982.

Blair, Helen. "A Thing 'of Shreds and Patches,'" *Ladies' Home Journal*, XIX (April 1902), 53.

Blair, Helen. "Collectors' Interests: Dower Chest Treasures," *House Beautiful*, XV (February 1904), 164.

"The Booming Business of Crafts: Will It Boomerang?," *Craft Horizons*, XXXIV (October 1974), 11 +.

Brackman, Barbara. *An Encyclopedia of Pieced Quilt Patterns.* Lawrence, Kansas: Prairie Flower Publications, 1979 (I), 1980 (II, III, IV), 1981 (V, VI), 1982 (VII), 1983 (VIII).

Brackman, Barbara. "Midwestern Pattern Sources," *Uncoverings 1980,* ed. Sally Garoutte. Mill Valley, Calif.: American Quilt Study Group, 1981.

Brackman, Barbara. "Patterns from the 1933 Chicago World's Fair," *Quilter's Newsletter Magazine,* XII (July/August 1981), 18–21.

Brackman, Barbara. "Quilts at Chicago's World's Fairs," *Uncoverings 1981*, ed. Sally Garoutte. Mill Valley, Calif.: American Quilt Study Group, 1982.

Brackman, Barbara. "Record Breaking Quilts," *Quilters' Journal,* V, xxi (1982), 5 +.

Brandt, Anthony. "A Short Natural History of Nostalgia," *Atlantic Monthly,* CCXLII (December 1978), 58–63.

Brown, Elsa. *Creative Quilting.* New York: Watson-Guptill Publications, 1975.

Bruce, Josephine. "Appliqué Patchwork," *Modern Priscilla,* August 1912, p. 13.

Bush, Donald J. *The Streamlined Decade.* New York: George Braziller, 1975.

Callahan, Nancy. "'Helping the Peoples to Help Themselves,'" *The Quilt Digest 4,* ed. Michael Kile. San Francisco: The Quilt Digest Press, 1986.

Callen, Anthea. *Women Artists of the Arts and Crafts Movement: 1870–1914.* New York: Pantheon Books, 1979.

Catalogue of . . . Quilts and Quilting: Attractive Applique Patchwork Designs with Border. St. Louis: Ladies Art Co., [n.d., c. 1930–1939].

Clark, Robert Judson, ed. *The Arts and Crafts Movement in America.* Catalogue for an exhibition organized by the Art Museum, Princeton University, and the Art Institute of Chicago, October 21–December 17, 1972.

Clarke, Gerald. "The Meaning of Nostalgia," *Time,* XCVII (May 3, 1971), 77.

Corbin, Patricia. "Notes to Help You Decorate It Yourself," *House & Garden,* CXLII (October 1972), 12 +.

"Craft Comeback, Folk Art, Decorative Inspiration: The All-American Patchwork Quilt," *House & Garden,* CXLII (October 1972), 114–117.

"Craze for Quilts," *Life,* LXXII (May 5, 1972), 74–80.

Cummins, Eleanor. "Blue and White," *The House Beautiful,* XVI (October 1904), 31–32.

Dennis, Landt. "Comeback of the Quilt," *Reader's Digest,* CII (March 1973), 35–38 +.

Designs Worth Doing. Independence, Mo.: McKim Studios, 1931.

Designs Worth Doing. Independence, Mo.: McKim Studios, Fall/Winter 1931–1932.

Doherty, M. Stephen. *Dynamic Still Lifes in Watercolor.* New York: Watson-Guptill Publications, 1983.

Emery, Elizabeth. "The Vital Things in the Home," *The House Beautiful,* XVI (October 1904), 13–14.

Emont-Scott, Deborah. *Alan Shields.* Memphis, Tenn.: Brooks Museum of Art, 1983.

Finley, Ruth E. *Old Patchwork Quilts and the Women Who Made Them.* Philadelphia: J. B. Lippincott Company, 1929.

Fisher, Karen. *Living for Today.* New York: A Studio Book, The Viking Press, 1972.

Foudji, Gazo. "A Dragon Bedquilt," *Ladies' Home Journal,* XXII (May 1905), 15.

Fox, Sandi. "The Log Cabin: An American Quilt on the Western Frontier," *The Quilt Digest 1,* ed. Roderick Kiracofe and Michael Kile. San Francisco: The Quilt Digest Press, 1983.

Glueck, Grace. "They're Shoofly and Crazy, Man," *The New York Times,* June 27, 1971, Sec. D, p. 24.

Godey's Lady's Magazine, October 1855.

Gouma-Peterson, Thalia, ed. *Miriam Schapiro: A Retrospective, 1953–1980.* Woos-ter, Ohio: The College of Wooster, 1980.

Grandma Dexter: New Applique and Patchwork Designs. Book no. 36B. Elgin, Ill.: Virginia Snow Studios, [n.d., c. 1927–1935].

Grandma Dexter's Applique and Patchwork Quilt Designs. Book no. 36. Elgin, Ill.: Virginia Snow Studios, [n.d., c. 1927–1935].

Grandmother Clark's Authentic Early American Patchwork Quilts. Book no. 23. St. Louis: W.L.M. Clark, Inc., 1932.

Grandmother Clark's Oldfashioned Quilt Designs. Book no. 21. St. Louis: W.L.M. Clark, Inc., 1931.

Grandmother Clark's Patchwork Quilt Designs. Book no. 20. St. Louis: W.L.M. Clark, Inc., 1931.

Grant, Helen. "Patches Gay in Every Way Make Your Bedroom Bright Each Day," *Needlecraft Magazine,* May 1923, p. 10.

Greif, Martin. *Depression Modern: The Thirties Style in America.* New York: Universe Books, 1975.

Gross, Joyce. "Bonnie Leman," *Quilters' Journal,* xx (1982), 1–4 +.

Hall, Carrie A., and Rose G. Kretsinger. *The Romance of the Patchwork Quilt in America.* New York: Bonanza Books, 1935.

Hammel, Lisa. "Crafts in Exurbia: Artisans Keep City at a Quiet Distance," *The New York Times,* March 5, 1970, p. 46.

Harp, Sybil C. "Quilt Makers Take Comfort in Revival," *The New York Times,* November 17, 1974, p. 39.

Heath, Frank. "Nostalgia Shock," *Saturday Review,* LIV (May 29, 1971), 18.

Hillier, Bevis. *Art Deco of the 20s and 30s.* New York: Schocken Books, 1985. Revision of 1968 edition.

Hillier, Bevis. *The Style of the Century: 1900–1980.* New York: E. P. Dutton, Inc., 1983.

Hillier, Bevis. *The World of Art Deco.* New York: E. P. Dutton, Inc., 1971.

"Hobbies Boom as Economy Fizzles," *The New York Times,* April 6, 1975, p. 33.

Holstein, Jonathan. "American Quilts as Visual Objects: A Personal View," *His-*

toric Preservation, XXIV (January/March 1972), 28–33.

Holstein, Jonathan. The Pieced Quilt: An American Design Tradition. Greenwich, Conn.: New York Graphic Society, Ltd., 1973.

Hooper, Bayard. "The Real Change Has Just Begun," Life, LXVIII (January 9, 1970), 102–106.

House & Garden, CXXXV–CXLIV (1969–1973).

[Advertisement for Patchcraft Corporation], House Beautiful, LXV (January 1929), 9.

House Beautiful, CXI–CXV (1969–1974).

"Jean Ray Laury," Quilters' Journal, II, iii (Fall 1979), 1–3.

Jenkins, Alan. The Thirties. New York: Stein and Day, 1976.

"The Joy of Quilting," Newsweek, LXXIX (January 10, 1972), 42.

King, Wayne. "The System's Dropouts Are Turning to Handicrafts in Search of New Values," The New York Times, November 24, 1970, p. 43.

Kramer, Hilton. "Art: Quilts Find a Place at the Whitney," The New York Times, July 3, 1971, p. 22.

Kramer, Hilton. "New Perspective on American Folk Art," The New York Times, February 1, 1974, p. 12.

Ladies' Home Journal, March 1885 and December 1904.

Lanigan, Sybil. "Revival of the Patchwork Quilt," Ladies' Home Journal, XI (October 1894), 19.

Lasansky, Jeannette. In the Heart of Pennsylvania: 19th and 20th Century Quiltmaking Traditions. Lewisburg, Penn.: Oral Traditions Project, 1985.

Laury, Jean Ray. Applique Stitchery. New York: Van Nostrand Reinhold Company, 1966.

Laury, Jean Ray. Quilts & Coverlets: A Contemporary Approach. New York: Van Nostrand Reinhold Company, 1970.

Leiser, Rabbi Joseph. "Simplicity: A Law of Nature," The Craftsman, August 1902, pp. 224–230.

Lewis, Alfred Allan. The Mountain Artisans Quilting Book. New York: Macmillan Publishing Co., Inc., 1973.

Lippard, Lucy. "Up, Down, and Across: A New Frame for New Quilts," The Artist and the Quilt, ed. Charlotte Robinson. New York: Alfred A. Knopf, 1983.

Lockwood, Sarah M. Decoration: Past, Present & Future. New York: The Literary Guild, 1934.

Lynes, Russell. The Tastemakers: The Shaping of American Popular Taste. New York: Dover Publications, Inc., 1980. Reprint of 1955 edition.

"Mail Order Catalogue of the Hip Becomes a National Best Seller," The New York Times, April 12, 1970, p. 67.

Malcolm, Janet. "On and Off the Avenue: About the House," The New Yorker, XLVII (September 4, 1971), 60–62.

Malcolm, Janet. "On and Off the Avenue: About the House," The New Yorker, L (September 2, 1974), 68–73.

McCrea, Margaret. "Good Ideas from Our Heritage of Quilts," Design, XLIV (November 1942), 8–10.

McCunn, Ethel M. "Quilting, an Old-Time Favorite and a Present-Day Fashion," Needlecraft Magazine, August 1926, p. 10.

McKim, Ruby. One Hundred and One Patchwork Patterns. New York: Dover Publications, Inc., 1962. Reprint of 1931 edition.

McMorris, Penny. Crazy Quilts. New York: E. P. Dutton, Inc., 1984.

McMorris, Penny. "Quilts in Art," The Quilt Digest 4, ed. Michael Kile. San Francisco: The Quilt Digest Press, 1986.

McMorris, Penny. "Victorian Style: Vintage Photographs of an American Home," The Quilt Digest 2, ed. Roderick Kiracofe and Michael Kile. San Francisco: The Quilt Digest Press, 1984.

Meikle, Jeffrey L. Twentieth Century Limited: Industrial Design in America, 1925–1939. Philadelphia: Temple University Press, 1979.

Mendes, Guy. "Appalachia Revisited," Craft Horizons, XXXVII (June 1977), 28–40+.

Morris, Bernadine. "Mountain Co-op Has a Rockefeller to Help Guide It," The New York Times, February 7, 1974, p. 32.

Mowry, George E., ed. The Twenties: Fords, Flappers & Fanatics. Englewood Cliffs, N.J.: Prentice-Hall, Inc., 1963.

Moyers, Bill. "Listening to America," Harper's, CCXLI (December 1970), 47–54+.

Naylor, Gillian. The Arts and Crafts Movement: A Study of Its Sources, Ideals, and Influence on Design Theory. Cambridge, Mass.: The M.I.T. Press, 1971.

Newell, Peter. "An Alice in Wonderland Bedquilt," Ladies' Home Journal, XXII (August 1905), 13.

"Nostalgia," Life, LXX (February 19, 1971), 39–78.

"Nostalgia," Newsweek, LXXVI (December 28, 1970), 34–38.

"Op: Adventure without Danger," Newsweek, LXV (March 1, 1965), 82–83.

Orlofsky, Patsy, and Myron Orlofsky. Quilts in America. New York: McGraw-Hill Book Company, 1974.

Parker, Rozsika, and Griselda Pollock. Old Mistresses: Women, Art and Ideology. New York: Pantheon Books, 1981.

Parrish, Maxfield. "A Circus Bedquilt," Ladies' Home Journal, XXII (March 1905), 11.

"Patchwork," Harper's Bazar, XV (September 16, 1882), 583.

Patchwork and Quilt Making. Newark, N.J.: Joseph Doyle & Co., [n.d., c. 1911].

"Patchwork: As American as Blue Jeans," House & Garden, CXXXIX (February 1971), 68–69.

"Patchwork Quilting: Coming into a Colorful Renascence," House Beautiful, CX (December 1968), 92–93.

Patchwork Quilts: How to Make Them. Chicago: Needlecraft Supply Co., 1938.

Paz, Octavio. In Praise of Hands: Contemporary Crafts of the World. Greenwich, Conn.: New York Graphic Society, Ltd., 1974.

"The Quest for Spiritual Survival," Life, LXVIII (January 9, 1970), 16–30.

Quilt Patterns: Patchwork and Applique. St. Louis: Ladies Art Co., 1928.

Quilter's Newsletter Magazine, March 1971–April 1985.

Reif, Rita. "If Only Liberace Would Quilt the Roof of His Car," The New York Times, June 25, 1971, p. 41.

Reif, Rita. "The Freedom Quilting Bee: A Cooperative Step Out of Poverty," *The New York Times,* July 9, 1968, p. 34.

Reif, Rita. "Quilting Co-op Tastes Success, Finds It Sweet," *The New York Times,* April 18, 1969, p. 47.

Robins, Corinne. "Anne Healy: Ten Years of Temporal Sculpture Outdoors and In," *Arts Magazine,* LIII (October 1978), 129–131.

"Ruby Short McKim: A Memorial," *Quilter's Newsletter Magazine,* VII (December 1976), 14–15.

Seton, Ernest Thompson. "A Wild-Animal Bedquilt," *Ladies' Home Journal,* XXII (January 1905), 9.

Sexton, Carlie. *Early American Quilts.* Southampton, N.Y.: Cracker Barrel Press, 1924.

Sexton, Carlie. *Old Fashioned Quilts.* Wheaton, Ill.: Carlie Sexton, 1928.

Sexton, Carlie. *Yesterday's Quilts in Homes of Today.* Des Moines, Iowa: Carlie Sexton, 1930.

Shannon, David A. *Between the Wars: America, 1919–1941.* Boston: Houghton Mifflin Company, 1979.

Shapiro, David. "American Quilts," *Craft Horizons,* XXXI (December 1971), 42–45.

Simon, Mrs. Leopold. "When Patchwork Becomes an Art," *Ladies' Home Journal,* XXV (August 1908), 45.

"A Stitch in Another Time," *Time,* LXXXVI (August 6, 1965), 60–61.

Thompson, Paul. *The Work of William Morris.* London: Quartet Books, 1977.

Tyrmand, Leopold. "Reflections: Revolution and Related Matters," *The New Yorker,* XLV (August 16, 1969), 40–75.

[Advertisement for Model Brassière Co.], *Vogue,* LXXIX (April 15, 1932), 106.

Weber, Eva. *Art Deco in America.* New York: Exeter Books, 1985.

Webster, Marie D. *Quilts: Their Story and How to Make Them.* Garden City, N.Y.: Doubleday, Page & Company, 1915.

"Wherever We Look, Something's Wrong," *Life,* LXIV (February 23, 1968), 4.

"Why the Craze for the 'Good Old Days,' " *U.S. News & World Report,* LXXV (November 12, 1973), 72–76.

INDEX

Italic figures denote pages with illustrations; bold figures denote plate numbers.

Additive approach to making art, 53–54

Agnew, Terese, **26**

Antiques, Colonial, collecting of, 29–30, 45, 49–50, 126 n. 21

Appliqué quilts, 27, 28, *28*, 31, 37, *37*, 58, *58*, 62

Art Deco, 33, 35–36; curvilinear designs, 36–37

Art quilt, see Quilt, art

Arts, fine vs. applied, 27, 35, 41: craft vs. art, 55–56

Arts and Crafts movement, 23–28, 30, 31, 41–42, 43; revival, 23, 41; interior design, *25,* 25–26; simplicity, 25–26; revival of cotton patchwork, 26–27; interest in the handmade, 41–42

Back-to-earth movement, 41–43, 45

Banham, Reyner, 42

Bates, David, 55, *57*

Batik, 66

Beneš, Barton, 54, *54,* 129 n. 105

Benglis, Lynda, 53

Berggruen Gallery, John, 47

Bicentennial, 51

Brand, Stewart, 41, 127 n. 63; *Whole Earth Catalog,* 41

Braque, Georges, 18, 53

Burbidge Pauline, 48, 60, 62, 63, 64, 66, 127 n. 66; **9, 16, 28**

Byrd, Admiral Richard Evelyn, 34

"Cabot Nancy," 35, 127 n. 36, 127 n. 38

Centennial Exposition (Philadelphia, 1876), 29

Chicago Tribune, 50, 127 n. 36

Chicago World's Fair (1933), 35

Christo, 53, 128 n. 101

"Circus Bedquilt, A," 28, *28*

Collage, 53, 54, *54,* 55, 129 n. 106

Colonial Pattern Co., 31

Colonial revival, *29,* 29–31, 32, 45, 126 n. 20; revival of cotton patchwork, 30, 31, 32; effect on quilt design, 30–32

Corcoran Gallery, James, 47

Crafts: revival in 1960's and 1970's, 40–43, 45, 49; department stores sell, 49

Craftsman, The, 25

Crazy quilts, 26, 31, 55–56, 58–59, *59,* 129 n. 107, 129n. 111, 129n. 112

Crossword puzzles, 34

Crow, Nancy, 43, 48, 49, 51–52, 60, 62, 63, 64, 69, *70–71;* **24**

Cyanotyping, 67

Day, Lewis F., 28

Depression, The, 34–35, 36, 37, 38, 49

Dove, Arthur, 53

Dyeing, 60, 66, *66*

Egyptian influence on design, 29, 32–33

Embroidery, 26, 27, 31, 36, 58, 60, 65, *65,* 126 n. 12, 126 n. 15

Ernst, Max, 53

Exhibitions, quilt, 43, 46–47, 51, 52, 128 n. 87, 128 n. 99, 128 n. 100, 129 n. 109: "The Artist & The Quilt," 52; Baltimore Museum of Art ("The Great American Cover-Up: Counterpanes of the 18th and 19th Centuries"), 128 n. 87; Berea (Ky.) College ("Patchwork Quilts of the Southern Highlands"), 128 n. 87; John Berggruen Gallery, 47; Chester County Historical Society, 128 n. 87; James Corcoran Gallery, 47; De Cordova (Lincoln, Mass.) Museum ("Bed and Board"), 128 n. 99: Monique Knowlton Gallery ("Edward Larson: Windtoys, Woodcarvings & Picture Quilts"), 129 n. 109: La Jolla (Calif.) Museum of Contemporary Art ("Artists Quilts"). 128 n. 100: The Museum of Contemporary Crafts ("The New American Quilt"), 51, 128 n. 99: Newark (N.J.) Museum ("Optical Quilts"), 47; Oakland (Calif.) Museum ("American Quilts: A Handmade Legacy"), 43; Pratt Graphics Center Gallery ("Printed Quilts, Quilted Prints"), 128 n. 99; Southeastern Ohio Cultural Arts Center ("Quilt National"), 52; Bernice Steinbaum Gallery ("The Decorative Aesthetic: Embroidered & Beaded Crazy Quilt & Screens"), 129 n. 109; Whitney Museum of American Art ("Abstract Design in American Quilts"), 46–47

Fabric as an art medium, 53, 56, 63, 64, 65, 69

Fabric Workshop, The, 129n. 116

Felix, Deborah, 60, 63, 67, 69, 129 n. 116; **22**

Feminism, 54–55, 61

Finley, Ruth E. *(Old Patchwork Quilts and the Women Who Made Them),* 30, 48

Fitzgerald, Veronica, *4, 67, 68,* 69; **23**

Fraas, Gayle, 51, 60, 62, 63, 66, 68; **4, 13**

Freckelton, Sondra, 54, 55

Gary, Belle, *28*

Godey's Lady's Book, 31

Good Housekeeping quilt contest, 51

"Grandma Dexter," 32, 38

"Grandmother Clark," 32, 127 n. 37

Gutcheon, Beth, 50

Hall, Carrie A., 33, 34, 38–39; and Rose G, Kretsinger (*The Romance of the Patchwork Quilt in America*), 33, 34

Headlee, Hannah Haynes, *37*

Healy, Anne, 53

Hewes, Jean, 50, 60, 64, *64*, 65, 66, 67, *67*: **2, 8, 12**

Holstein, Jonathan, 46

Home Art Studios, 31

House & Garden, 44, 50, *50*

House Beautiful, 25, 27, 44, 127 n. 56, 128 n. 87

Impressionists, 42, 64

Indian designs, influence on quilts, 33, *33*

Industrial design, 35, 36

James, Michael, 43, 44, 48, 60, 62, 63–64, 69, 128 n. 99; **1, 14**

Johns, Jasper, 53

Kansas City Star, The, 34, *34*, 35, *35*, 127 n. 37, 127 n. 38

Katzenberg, Dena, 128 n. 87

Kaufman, Jane, 55–56, *59*, 129 n. 109

Kiracofe, Roderick, 48

Kramer, Hilton, 46

Kretsinger, Rose G., see Hall, Carrie A.

Ladies Art Co., 31, *31*, 127 n. 56

Ladies' Home Journal, 26, 27, 28, *28*, 126 n. 17

Laury, Jean Ray, 43, 47, 50

Leiser, Rabbi Joseph, 41

Lichtenstein, Roy, 53

Lindbergh, Charles, 34

Lintault, M. Joan, **27**

Lockport Cotton Batting Company, 33

Lynes, Russell, 36

MacConnel, Kim, 129 n. 116

MacLeish, Archibald, 128 n. 81

Mangat, Terrie Hancock, *1, 2, 10–11*, 42, 49, 51, 59, 60, 63, 65, *65*, 66–67, *67*: **6, 15, 25**

May, Therese, 5, 60, 64, 65–66, *66*, 67: **3, 20**

McCall's Needlework and Crafts, 49

McDowell, Ruth, *20–21*, 64, 66, 68: **10**

McKim, Ruby, 35–36, *36*, 48, 127 n. 48, 127 n. 53, 129 n. 114: *One Hundred and One Patchwork Patterns*, 36, 48, 127 n. 48

McKim Studios, 31, 36; *Designs Worth Doing*, 36, *36*

McMorris, Penny (*Crazy Quilts*), 18

Metropolitan Museum of Art (New York City), 29

Missouri Historical Society, 129 n. 113

Morris, William, 25

Moyers, Bill, 40

Museum of Modern Art (New York City) ("Machine Art"), 127 n. 46

Myers-Newbury, Jan, *3*, 60, 62, 63, 66, *66*, 68, 69; **19**

Nagin, Risë, 49, 63, 65, 66, 67; **18**

Needlecraft Magazine, 28, *29*

Needlecraft Supply Co., 32, 127 n. 56

Newark (N.J.) Museum, 127 n. 46; "Optical Quilts," 47

Newspaper columns, syndicated quilt, 32–35

Nochlin, Linda, 129 n. 107

Norvell, Patsy, 129 n. 107

Oldenburg, Claes, 53

Op Art, 47

Painting (on quilts), 60, 64, *65*, 65–66, *66*; with dyes, 66

Parish-Hadley, 44

Parrish, Maxfield ("A Circus Bedquilt"), 28, *28*

Pattern painters, 17, 54, *55*, *56*, 59, 64, 65, 129 n. 116

Patterns, quilt, see Quilt patterns

Photocopying, 60, 66

Picasso, Pablo, 18, 53

Plotkin, Linda, 55, *56*

Pop Art, 47, 51, 52, 53

Porcella, Yvonne, *12*, 59, 62, 64, 65, 66, 68; **7**

Prairie Farmer, 127 n. 36

Progressive Farmer, 127 n. 38

Quilt art: traditional vs. art quilt controversy, 58–59, 60–61, 69; differs from traditional quilts, 60, 68; effect of movement upon quiltmaking, 61–62, 69; large scale of, 68; three-dimensional forms, *12*, 68; **4, 7, 13**; three-dimensional projections, *20–21*, 68; **10**; free-hanging, double-sided, 68; **11, 17**

Quilt, art, techniques: three-dimensional embellishments and forms, 59, *64*, 65, *67*; photocopying, 60, 66; embroidery, 60, 65, *65*; painting, 60, 64, *65*, 65–66, *66*; stenciling and stamping, 60, 67; dyeing, 60, 66, *66*; transparent fabric over dense, 64, *64*, 67; adding canvas, 65; staining, 66; painting with dyes, 66; batik, 66; loose threads, *66*; 67: cyanotyping, 67; unfinished edges, 67, *67*; reversed fabric, 67; thin fabric over broad, 67, *68*

Quilt artists: training and academic backgrounds, 61; influence on quiltmaking, 61–62; economic survival, 62; appeal of fabric, 63; sewing backgrounds, 63; quiltmaking relatives, 63; appeal of construction process, 63–64; audience, 69

Quilt co-operatives, 42, 43, 44, 128 n. 71; Blue Ridge Hearthside Crafts Association, 128 n. 71; Cabin Creek Quilts, 42, 128 n. 71; Dakotah Handcrafts, 128 n. 71: Freedom Quilting Bee, 44, 128 n. 71; Mountain Artisans, 42, 43, 44, 128 n. 71

Quilt design, movement away from originality, 30–36, 38, 51

Quilt patterns, 30–36, 38: *The Airplane*, *34*, 127 n. 38; *Air-Ship Propeller*, *34*, 127 n 38; *Arrowheads*, 127 n. 37; *Bridge Quilt*, 34, *35*; *Byrd at the South Pole*, 34; *The Chief*, *33*; *Cleopatra's Puzzle*, 127 n. 36; *Crossword Puzzle*, 34; *Depression*, 35; *Double Irish Chain*, 127 n. 56; *Double Wedding Ring*, 37, 127 n. 37; *Dresden Plate*, *37*; *Economy*, 35; *Egyptian Butterfly*, 33; *The Four Winds*, 34; *Grandmother's Flower Garden*, 37; *Hard Times Block*, 35; *Indian Canoes*, 127 n. 37; *Indian Mats*, 127 n 37; *Indian Maze*, 127 n. 37; *Indian Square*, 127 n. 37; *Indian Trail*, 127 n. 37; *Indian Wedding Ring*, 127 n. 37; *Iris*, 36, *37*; *King Tut's Crown*, 127 n. 36; *Lindbergh's Night Flight*, 127 n. 38; *Lindy's Plane*, 127 n. 38; *Log Cabin*, 44, 54, 58, 128 n. 104, 129 n. 112; *Ma Perkins Flower Garden*, 34; *Mohawk Trail*, 127 n. 37; *Navajo* 127 n.

37; *Poppy*, 36; *Robbing Peter to Pay Paul*, 127 n. 36; *Spirit of St. Louis*, 127 n. 38; *Swastika*, *33*; *Thrifty*, 35; *The Thrifty Wife*, 35; *Trumpet Vine*, 36

Quilter's Newsletter Magazine, 43, 46, 50

Quilts: as art objects, 27, 46–47, 57–58, 129 n. 110; collecting, 18, 27, 30, 45, 47–48; change in status, 18, 27, 52, 54–55; movement from beds to walls. 18, *50*, 57; crazy quilts, 26, 31, 55–56, 58–59, *59*, 129 n. 111, 129 n. 112; appliqué, 27, 28, *28*, 31, 37, *37*, 58, *58*, 62; kits, 31, 36, 38–39, 51, 127 n. 56; pictured and promoted in the press, 44–45, 47, 48, 50, *50*: rise in prices, 47–48, 49, 50; growth in number of dealers, 47; similarities with modern art designs, 47, 57; Amish, 48; influence in art, 53, 54, 54–56, *55*, *56*, 57, *58*, *59*; traditional vs. contemporary, 58–59, 60–61, 69

Rauschenberg, Robert, 54, *54*

Rockburne, Dorothea, 128 n. 104

Rosenquist, James, 53

Ruskin, John, 42, 127 n. 66

Schapiro, Miriam, 54, 55, *55*, 56, 69, 129 n. 106, 129 n. 116

Schirm, David, 55, *57*

Schulze, Joan, *8*, 59, 60, 63, 64, 66, 67, 68; **11, 17**

Sears, Roebuck, 35, 127 n. 56

Segal, George, 53

Seton, Ernest Thompson, 126 n. 17

Shapiro, David, 46

Shields, Alan, 53, *53*

Slade, Duncan, *9*, 51, 60, 62, 63, 66, 68; **4, 13**

Small, Albert, 34

Staining, 66

Stamping, 60, 67

Stearns & Foster, 44

Steinbaum, Bernice, 69

Stella, Frank, 47

Stenciling, 60, 67

"Streamlining," 36, *36*

Studstill, Pamela, 49, 60, 64 65, *65*; **5, 21**

Three-dimensional embellishments, 59, *64*, 65, *67*

Tyrmand, Leopold, 45

Valerio, James, 55, *58*

Van der Hoof, Gail, 46

Vasarély, Victor, 47

Virginia Snow Studios, 32

Vogue, 37, 44

Vreeland, Diana, 44

Warhol, Andy, 53

Webster, Marie (*Quilts: Their Story and How to Make Them*), 27

West Virginia, encouragement of crafts, 42–43

Wharton, Margaret, 55, *58*

Wilson, Ann, 54